Dyslexia and Reading
A Neuropsychological Approach

Dyslexia and Reading

A Neuropsychological Approach

JEAN ROBERTSON BEd, MEd, PhD

Senior Lecturer in Special Education, Manchester Metropolitan University

Consultant in Dyslexia

Professor Margaret Snowling, University of York

W

WHURR PUBLISHERS

LONDON AND PHILADELPHIA

© 2000 Whurr Publishers
First published 2000 by
Whurr Publishers Ltd
19b Compton Terrace, London N1 2UN, England and
325 Chestnut Street, Philadelphia PA106, USA

British Library Cataloguing in Publication Data
A catalogue record for this book is available from the
British Library.

ISBN 1 86156 136 9

Printed and bound in the UK by Athenaeum Press Ltd,
Gateshead, Tyne & Wear

Contents

Dedication

This book is dedicated to my children.

Acknowledgements

Acknowledgement is made of the contribution of Professor Peter D. Pumfrey (Victoria University of Manchester), who meticulously supervised my original research in this area and provided support and encouragement throughout. Also I should like to acknowledge the contribution of Professor Dirk J. Bakker (Free University of Amsterdam). Since I first visited him in 1994, he has given generously of his time, supplying much advice and encouragement. Other acknowledgement goes to the teachers who took part in the original research, to my current students, whose interest and enthusiasm are magnificent, and to the pupils with whom I have worked and from whom I have learned so much.

I should also like to thank Whurr Publishers for their help during the preparation of this book. Similar acknowledgement goes to Peter Nathan for permission to use certain of his illustrations and to Uta Frith for permission to use a model of the biological basis of dyslexia. The original illustrations are the work of Ted Bates (Artbox).

Finally I should like to acknowledge the support given by my husband Robert, both during the research projects, upon which this volume is based, and while completing this volume. The positive help given both in encouragement and endless proofreading was invaluable.

Preface

There is currently much interest in the field of dyslexia from many different perspectives. Much of the research centres on the aetiology of this complex disorder, and scientific advances are contributing to knowledge of the subject at a significant rate. However, very little research is carried out into effective intervention even though this is an area which could benefit people with dyslexia directly. Study of the neuropsychological implications of dyslexia may usefully form one bridge between theory and practice.

This book is intended for all those teachers responsible for teaching students with dyslexia and for research students in this field. It is hoped that it will add another perspective to intervention. The book begins with an overview of neuropsychological theory and brain function. Though complex, the theory may be effective in shedding light on what practitioners observe in their day-to-day interaction with students. This is discussed in relation to the varied demands of the reading process and to an overview of how neuropsychological theory contributes to the development of specific intervention techniques. The following chapters are devoted to both practical and theoretical considerations. It is hoped that the neuropsychological perspective will make a contribution to the range of strategies currently available for students with dyslexia and may be effective in addressing some of their needs in relation to the attainment of literacy.

Chapter 1
Neuropsychology and reading

Introduction

When the various elements within the reading process are analysed, many different skills and abilities are found to be necessary for fluent and successful reading. The extent of the interest generated by this complex activity is revealed by examination of different theories of reading. A wide variety of different theories are also found when the various brain functions involved in the reading process are investigated. The topic of reading attracts workers from various disciplines and different standpoints. Psychologists may be interested in the cognitive processes utilized in reading, whereas teachers may be more interested in how successful reading can be readily accomplished by pupils. Neuropsychologists may be interested in the brain regions that are activated in the complex process of reading.

Perception of the reading task impacts on research methodology. Research interest is generated by the study of how the brain of a successful reader accomplishes the reading task easily and how the process fails for others. Both perspectives present a challenge to the researcher and currently there is much research interest in the successful as well as the failing reader. The neuropsychological perspective can be used to consider both positions and the historical background of the study of specific locations for specific brain functions can provide a useful starting point. This study has a long history but is still generating research interest.

Background to neuroanatomy

The background to the neuropsychological investigation of reading begins with the study of the different parts of the brain and their respective contribution to certain aspects of behaviour. All the brain regions reported are located on the cortex. The cortex (the Latin word for the bark of a tree) or neocortex – the terms can be used interchangeably – comprises most of the forebrain and consists of four to six layers of grey matter; any brain area composed mainly of cell bodies is grey matter. The cortex makes up 80% of the human brain. It is a wrinkled structure,

1

approximately 2mm thick. The wrinkled structure of the cortex consists of clefts and ridges. These effectively increase the surface area while still containing the structure within the relatively small human skull. A deep cleft is called a fissure and a shallow cleft is called a sulcus (plural sulci). A ridge is called a gyrus (plural gyri). The cortex is divided into two hemispheres and each hemisphere is split into four 'lobes, with the divisions marked by folds. At the very back of the brain is the occipital lobe; the part around the ears is the temporal lobe; the top section is the parietal lobe; and in front of that is the frontal lobe (see Figure 1.1).

Each of the lobes has specific responsibilities and functions. The occipital lobe contains the visual processing areas; the parietal lobe deals with movement, orientation, calculation and body senses; the temporal lobes deal with auditory perception, sound and speech comprehension; and the frontal lobes integrate most mental processes. The frontal lobes are considered to be the location of the higher order skills of thinking, conceptualizing and planning. Below the four sections lies the cerebellum, which is sometimes referred to as the little brain. This is responsible for balance, movement and equilibrium.

Many of the structures on the brain are labelled according to their location in relation to the other structures. Conventionally six terms are used to indicate anatomical direction: superior (top), lateral (side), medial (middle), ventral (bottom), anterior (front) and posterior (back).

Generally the surface features of the brain may have certain differences but the main sulci and gyri will be common to all and are used as landmarks to describe various regions on the brain.

The nervous system is arranged symmetrically and has two hemispheres. If two structures are on the same side they are ipsilateral; if on opposite sides they are contralateral; and if they are on both sides they are referred to as bilateral.

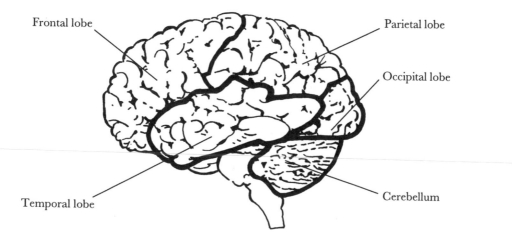

Figure 1.1 The sections of the brain.

Certain brain areas are known to be important in the study of both language and reading. These include Broca's area, Wernicke's area, the corpus callosum, the angular gyrus, the arcuate fasciculus, the visual cortex, the cerebellum and the insular cortex (see Figure 1.2). All of these cortical (situated on the cortex) areas have been studied in relation to dyslexia and have the following functions.

Broca's area is found in the temporal lobes at the side of the frontal lobes. It is alongside the motor cortex and is implicated in the movement of the jaw, larynx, tongue and lips necessary for speech production.

Wernicke's area, found at the back of the temporal lobe next to the parietal lobe, is involved in speech comprehension.

The **corpus callosum** is a fibre system connecting the two hemispheres of the brain and is responsible for the smooth transfer of information from one hemisphere to the other.

The **angular gyrus** is a gyrus in the edges of the occipital (vision), parietal (spatial skills) and temporal (language) lobe and is important in linking the visual word recognition system to the phonological or sound system.

The **arcuate fasciculus** is a long bundle of fibres linking Broca's area for language production to Wernicke's area for language comprehension.

The **visual cortex** is located in the occipital lobe and is responsible for the visual processes.

The **cerebellum** is situated at the bottom of the cortex. Though separate from the cortex it is partly fused to it. This is implicated in balance, co-ordination and language.

The **insular cortex** is found in a fold within Broca's area and is believed to be a bridge between the language areas, which effectively orchestrates the activity of the different areas.

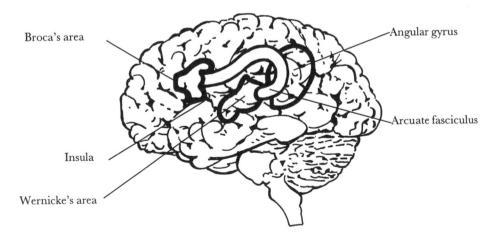

Figure 1.2 The major language areas of the brain.

All of these areas are involved in the ongoing research into dyslexia but certain of them also have a long history in the literature of dyslexia.

An historical perspective

Records of work on dyslexia can be traced back to the eighteenth and nineteenth centuries and particularly the work of Gall and Spurzheim in the early 1800s on phrenology (long discredited study of the relationship between mental faculties and the surface features of the skull). They found that the connection from the cortex (most of the forebrain) to the spinal cord could demonstrate the link between brain and behaviour. They also recognized the connection between the two hemispheres by the corpus callosum. From this anatomical basis they developed a theory of how the brain produces behaviour and how different areas of the cortex have different functions (see Figure 1.3).

Gall considered language function to be localized in the frontal lobe and this stimulated the work of Jean Baptiste Bouillaud. In 1825, he read a paper before the Royal Academy of Medicine in France and presented clinical studies showing that function is localized in the neocortex and speech in the frontal lobes. This supported the Gall theory of language being based mainly in the frontal lobe and led to the work of Paul Broca, which eventually led to a region

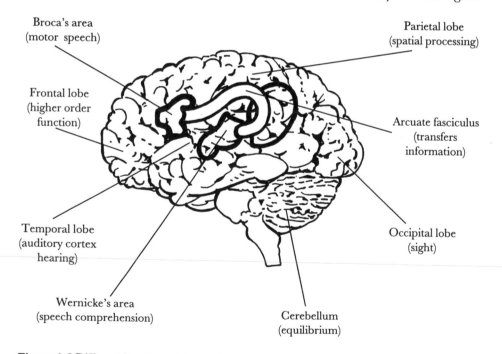

Broca's area
(motor speech)

Parietal lobe
(spatial processing)

Frontal lobe
(higher order
function)

Arcuate fasciculus
(transfers
information)

Temporal lobe
(auditory cortex
hearing)

Occipital lobe
(sight)

Wernicke's area
(speech comprehension)

Cerebellum
(equilibrium)

Figure 1.3 Different functions of the cortical areas.

in the left frontal lobe being named 'Broca's area'. Resultant damage to this area was termed 'Broca's aphasia', aphasia being a defect or loss of power of expression by speech, writing or signs, or of comprehending spoken or written language due to injury or disease of the brain (Kolb and Whishaw 1996). Evidence for this came from 25 post-mortem studies on subjects with aphasia. One of the subjects was the patient 'Tan', thus named due to an inability to use any other language than the simple phrase 'Tan, Tan'. Following his death, post-mortem investigation revealed damage to the left hemisphere. This contributed to the concept of cerebral dominance and the idea that the different hemispheres have different functions.

The work of Broca led to two basic ideas: that a specific brain area controls specific behaviour such as language and that damage to the area destroys that behaviour. Several theorists disagreed with such a strict notion of localization. One influential dissenter was Carl Wernicke. He suggested there was more than one language area and that deficits in specific areas did not inevitably result in damage to language function.

Wernicke subsequently provided a model of sequential processing of language. He wrote that the sound image of objects is stored in an area of the cortex (subsequently known as Wernicke's area) and then sent via a pathway (a long bundle of fibres linking the two areas, later known as the arcuate fasciculus) to Broca's area, which retains the representations for speech movements. He suggested that if the fibres connecting the two speech areas were damaged, conduction aphasia – a type of fluent aphasia in which, despite alleged normal comprehension of spoken language, words are repeated incorrectly - would result (Kolb and Whishaw 1996). The idea of disconnection was important as it predicted that deficit would follow either disconnection or damage to an area. The work was influential in stimulating further study and served as a basis for the work of Geschwind in the 1960s. Figure 1.4 shows an overview of the various processes involved in processing a heard stimulus.

The Wernicke–Geschwind model

The Wernicke–Geschwind model proposes that the primary auditory cortex receives the original auditory stimulus and projects it to Wernicke's area, where the word is analysed for meaning. The information is then projected to Broca's area, which contains the memory of the motor programmes necessary for word articulation. Ultimately the facial area of the motor cortex receives input from Broca's area and facilitates articulation of the word. Different processes are found when the word is accessed via the visual modality. If the text is read silently, the primary visual association cortex receives the input and projects it to Wernicke's area, where the auditory form of the word is activated and comprehension occurs. Figure 1.5 shows the processes evoked by seeing a word.

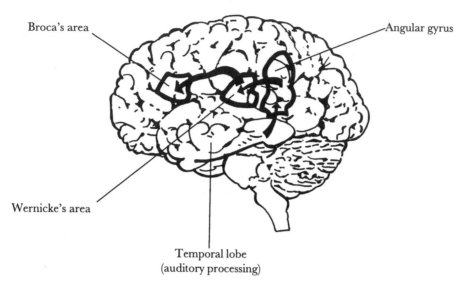

Figure 1.4 A model of brain activity in hearing words.

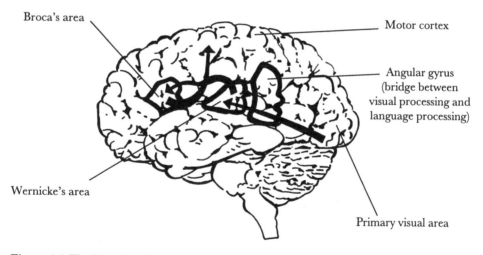

Figure 1.5 The Wernicke–Geschwind model for reading words aloud.

Technological advances now provide further evidence of the complex activity of the brain in the reading process, and current thinking about the localization of language processes is the result of magnetic resonance imaging (MRI) studies, lesion studies (damage to the nervous system) and electrophysiological studies. An excellent overview of the various investigation techniques is provided in Carter (1998). The MRI technique aligns atomic particles in the tissue by magnetism and then bombards them with radio waves. The bombarded particles emit radio signals, which differ according to the type of tissue present. The use of a complex software program (computerized tomography or CT) converts this into a 3D image of the part of the body under investigation. The result is an 'X-ray picture' of the soft tissue.

Many studies of brain and language function extend this technique by the use of functional MRI (fMRI). This can extend the basic picture by revealing the areas of greatest brain activity. Glucose and oxygen, both of which are carried in the blood, fuel neuronal firing. When an area of the brain is activated, these substances flow towards it and the fMRI can demonstrate the areas that have most oxygen, depending on the amount of activity. Modern scans are now capable of producing images every four seconds so that any changes in activity according to the task demands are revealed. This capacity makes fMRI one of the most promising of the new techniques but unfortunately it has the disadvantage of being very expensive.

Another approach, which can give similar results, is positron emission topography (PET). These scans are also successful in identifying the brain areas most involved in a given task by measuring the fuel consumed. A central problem with this technique is that it is an invasive technique. It requires the injection of a radioactive marker into the bloodstream, which is metabolized by the brain and subsequently recorded by a special detector. Though the dosage of radiation is minimal, there is a limit to the number of sessions a person may receive over the course of a year and in most cases this is limited to 12.

Electrophysiological studies (either electroencephalogram, EEG, or event-related potential, ERP) measure brain activity by placing electrodes at strategic points on the skull. The ERP technique presents a stimulus (either visual or auditory) to the person undergoing the EEG and measures the type of activity generated. ERP studies have the advantage of being non-invasive but unfortunately cannot provide the quality of information generated by the more sophisticated fMRI technique.

Other techniques which may ultimately contribute to a better understanding of the complexity of the brain activity involved in reading are currently being developed. In some instances the study of abnormal reading behaviour (as in some dyslexic subjects) is by post-mortem studies; and research by this means is also ongoing.

Research so far has demonstrated the importance of not just the classic language areas of Broca and Wernicke but the contribution of many brain regions to the complex process of reading. Two important elements in this process are both the visual and auditory channels through which the brain receives the initial stimuli.

The brain and visual perception

The visual pathway is the name of the route by which nerve impulses travel from the eye through the brain to the right and left visual cortex at the rear. When light falls on the retina it triggers a chemical reaction within the cells. This is converted into a nerve impulse passed out from the back of the eye by the optic nerve. The right and left optic nerves run in a posterior (front to back) direction and meet at the optic chiasma, which is a crossing point central to the process of visual perception. Here, crossing is a partial process, as fibres from the inside half of each eye cross to the opposite side of the brain. (This is an example of the crossover process of the brain and body relationship. Thus the left side of the body is governed by the right side of the brain and the right side of the body by the left side of the brain.) In the optic chiasma the two sets of optic nerves (optic tracts) continue to run through the brain to the lateral geniculate nucleus and ultimately reach the visual area of the brain located in the occipital cortex. The left optic tract deals with information from the outside half of the left eye and the inside half of the right eye. The right optic tract deals with information from the inside half of the left eye and the outside half of the right eye (see Figure 1.6).

The brain and auditory perception

The auditory cortex is normally thought of as being in the temporal lobe, which is an area found laterally on the brain below the lateral sulci adjacent to the temporal bones. In reality the auditory cortex extends into the parietal lobe. The main areas for auditory perception are found in the temporal bank of the Sylvian or lateral fissure, which is a deep cleft separating the temporal and parietal lobes (see Figure 1.7).

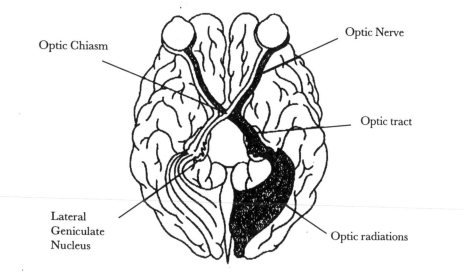

Figure 1.6 showing the visual pathway.

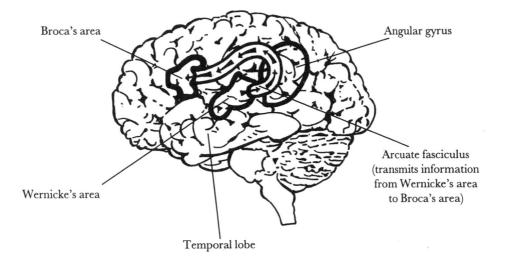

Broca's area

Angular gyrus

Arcuate fasciculus
(transmits information
from Wernicke's area
to Broca's area)

Wernicke's area

Temporal lobe

Figure 1.7 The auditory pathway.

Auditory projections (sounds) are heard in the primary cortex and are relayed to the secondary auditory cortex, known as the planum temporale, and the superior temporal gyrus. This is the site where auditory phonemes or speech sounds arc mapped on to the visual graphemes; these being letters or clusters of letters that can be decoded without being sounded out. There is evidence that the right hemisphere normally mediates non-verbal or visuospatial processing. Within the field of dyslexia the planum temporale has been the focus of much study and will be discussed in greater detail later in the chapter (see Figure 1.8).

The processes involved in both vision and hearing demonstrate the crossover of stimuli from one side to the other. In both cases nerve impulses travel along nerve fibres which divide into two. Some of the impulses travel to the opposite side of the brain but some remain on the same side. For most right-handed people, language is interpreted mainly in the left hemisphere so this hemisphere becomes dominant for language and it can be seen that in right-handed people the planum temporale is usually larger in the left hemisphere (see Figure 1.9).

Cases where the planum temporale is not larger in the left hemisphere have revealed exceptional development of visuospatial ability but poorer phonological or other language skills.

The brain and language

The study of the brain and language has a central role within the study of reading. One is the medium by which the other is attained; many reading processes can be seen as linguistic processes.

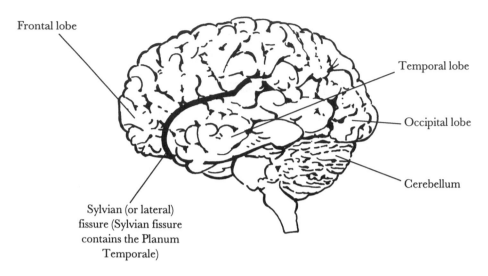

Figure 1.8 The Sylvian (or lateral) fissure and the Planum Temporale.

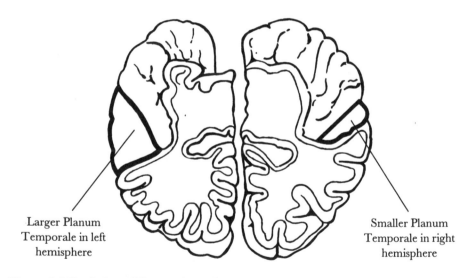

Figure 1.9 Hemisphere differences in the Planum Temporale.

Knowledge of this field was advanced by the work of Canadian neurosurgeon Wilder Penfield, who, in the 1950s, charted large regions of the cerebral cortex by applying electrodes to different areas of the brains of hundreds of patients with epilepsy (Penfield and Roberts 1959).

These studies by Penfield and his associates were among the first to identify the speech zones. Experimentally they provided evidence that stimulation of a number of cortical areas with a low voltage electrical current interferes with speech. The areas included the cortical areas of Broca and Wernicke in the left hemisphere as well as the sensory and motor representations of the face and supplementary speech area in both hemispheres. Specific effects included word retrieval or naming difficulties arising from stimulation of Broca's (anterior or frontal) region or Wernicke's (posterior) region. Thus a person with naming difficulties might ask 'Could I have that thing to write with please?' instead of 'Could I have that pen?'; there was also a tendency to describe objects by function instead of by name. Other effects here included semantic substitutions, such as substituting the word 'house' for 'home'. Stimulation also disturbed the ability to perform phonemic discrimination tasks, for example patients could not respond accurately to the question 'Do the words pig and big begin with the same letter?'.

Other studies found gender differences in the size of the language area between males and females (Ojemann and Mateer 1979). In males, the language area is larger than in females. This was surprising in view of the popular perception of the generally superior verbal skills of females. Their conclusion was that the size of the language area might be inversely related to ability and that more effective areas may actually be distributed over a smaller cortical area than weaker functions. Ojemann supported this conclusion with other studies with multilingual subjects, where he found that the poorer language area is generally distributed over a larger area than the stronger one. Kolb and Whishaw (1996) concluded that improved efficiency requires less rather than more neuronal activity and that 'smart brains work better not harder'. Ojemann's work also provided evidence that stimulation at particular points on the cortex has very specific effects and that, for example, stimulation of one site will impact on one aspect of language (for example, naming ability) on every trial but will leave other language functions intact.

The Ojemann and Mateer studies also demonstrated that the language areas are not so strictly localized and the work corrected some previous misconceptions, for example the widespread belief that damage to Broca's area results in deficits in language production only. Left frontal lesions in the vicinity of Broca's area did not only impact on speech production but were also found to produce associated deficits in comprehension. Stimulation of the speech zones affected more than just talking, as deficits were also found in voluntary control of the face muscles and short-term memory and reading. Facial lesions were found to impair abilities in both spelling and differentiating between heard sounds.

These and other studies demonstrate the importance of specific locations and of the links between the regions. They may also be seen to demonstrate how performance on certain tasks may be implicated by damage to both specific and diverse areas. Task demands can impact on experimental results and this provides another route by which the links between tasks and brain regions can be investigated. This is demonstrated by the ERP studies which now show differences in processing environmental sounds versus speech-like sounds, and single words versus connected text (Van Patten and Rheinfelder 1995). They concluded that non-linguistic sounds are processed differently. These various studies may indicate that the activity generated and the brain regions involved may differ according to the task demands. To understand this it is useful to consider the various stages involved in processing a single word.

Stages in processing single words

When a word is presented visually, Kolb and Whishaw (1996) describe the varied activities undertaken. Initially the surface visual features of the word can be inspected and decoded. Then the phonological aspects of the word can be considered. These include analysis of letter sounds at the beginning and end of the word and whether rhymes are possible. Thus both the visual and auditory surface features of the word are analysed. Consideration is then given to the semantics or the meaning of the word. A question of some debate has been whether these three levels of analysis are done in series (sequentially) or in parallel. If done sequentially the words must be visually inspected and then sounded before they are understood. There is the implication that non-words that can be pronounced, for example 'jep', must be analysed differently than non-words that are not pronounceable, for example 'xtv'. If the brain activity generated is found to be different, there is some evidence for serial processing.

One way this was studied was by investigation into regional blood flow to the different brain regions. This could demonstrate one element of the reading process. This was investigated by Petersen et al. (1988) and Posner and Raichle (1994), and differences in brain activity were found according to the precise nature of the task the subjects were required to undertake. In a passive task of merely processing words presented visually or auditorally there was increased blood flow bilaterally in the primary and secondary visual areas when seeing a word. When hearing a word the blood flow increased in the primary and secondary auditory areas. Words and non-words that could be pronounced activated a region in the left occipital cortex. The same region was not activated by letter strings that could not be pronounced. This could indicate that the brain processes visual aspects such as letters that are related to language differently from other purely visual stimuli such as a series of geometric shapes (see Figure 1.10).

This study suggested an initial classification process into word versus non-word. Both words and non-words that were pronounceable activated Wernicke's area, whereas listening to simple tones and vowels did not. As this will depend to some extent upon previous experience of language it may suggest that some elements may be dependent on the subject's exposure to print and word-like forms.

This study did not show evidence of overlap between the visual and auditory modalities because processing of the words was completed independently. This

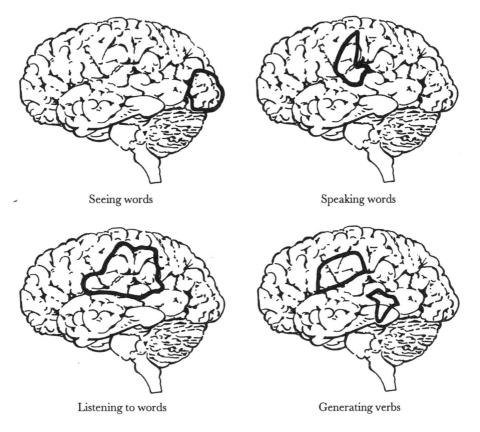

Seeing words

Speaking words

Listening to words

Generating verbs

(After Posner and Raichle, 1994)

Figure 1.10 Differential brain activity demonstrated by different tasks.

contradicts the view of language comprehension that suggests that visual analysis is followed by a phonological or letter sound-based analysis by a serial process. However, when the task was changed to a word repetition task, requiring enunciation rather than reading words aloud, there was bilateral activation of the motor and sensory face areas, the supplementary speech area and the right cerebellum. There was also activation of the insular cortex. A surprising result was that neither Broca's nor Wernicke's area was activated during the repetition task.

The research of Petersen et al. (1988) also suggests that orthographic (written) and phonological (sound) information is represented by different neural structures. Differences have also been found according to the grammatical class of the stimulus. One example of this is that the verb/noun distinction appears to be distributed along the anterior/posterior axis of the language area. One theory is that the systems that mediate between concepts and nouns are located in the left temporal area while equivalent systems for concepts and verbs could be located in the left frontal area. There is a question mark over how much credence can be given to work based on single case studies, but case study research can enable the formulation and ultimate testing of new hypotheses to take place.

Thus task demands have been found significant in many studies. The brain regions implicated have also been found to differ according to word classes, for example function or closed class words such as 'he', 'she' and 'but' and open class words such as 'tea', 'go' and 'green'. Even finer distinctions have been found to have impact. These include work on the processing of real words or letter strings, the impact of presentation rate or the high or low frequency of words. The studies by Petersen et al. (1988) also noted other effects. If the noun 'cake' was presented visually, vocalizing the verb 'eat' resulted in activation of the left frontal lobe. Silent verb generation activated the supplementary motor area and the part of the brain which includes Broca's area (motor area for speech). Individual differences were found, as in one case frontal gyri were particularly affected in the naming and comprehension of verbs.

Split brain research (where the two hemispheres are artificially separated by severing the corpus callosum) has provided evidence of receptive language abilities in an isolated right hemisphere, especially of short and concrete content words (Coslett and Monsul 1994). Such studies have led to the belief that each hemisphere may have its own lexicon or dictionary or store of known words. This is not to say that the involvement of each hemisphere would be equivalent, and it may depend on such factors as the type of words. Words having a tangible meaning, or content words, could be found in both hemispheres but function words would be located only in the left hemisphere. Input to the right hemisphere would be possible only after involvement of the left hemisphere. This would mean that content words presented in either visual half-field could be processed by either hemisphere, but function words would be accessed by the right hemisphere (if presented to the left visual field/right hemisphere) only after involvement and relay via the corpus callosum. An important question is whether the hemispheres act independently or co-operatively, and research into this question is ongoing. This will be discussed in greater detail later in this chapter.

Another area that showed differential activation according to aspects of the task involved was the role of the insular cortex, and differences were found according to whether the task involved immediate word retrieval (for example naming pictures) or involved material which the subjects had been given the opportunity to practise. In a word-retrieval task the role of the insular cortex was not increased. It was, however, enhanced when subjects had an opportunity to practise their response. In this event the role of the insular was enhanced whereas the activity of the other regions ceased. The insular was implicated only when a practised response was required (Paulesu et al. 1996).

These studies indicate the involvement of areas other than the classic anterior (Broca's area) and posterior (Wernicke's) speech zones. They also suggest that the posterior speech zone may be devoted largely to the analysis of auditory input, as there was no increase in blood flow in the area usually stimulated by visual stimuli. Additionally they may cast doubt on the traditional view of Broca's area as being simply a cortical representation of the movement of speech, as this may depend on additional factors such as whether the response is novel or learned. If learned, the insula would also be implicated.

Evidence that contributes to the neuropsychological theory has also been obtained by the study of brain lesions. Many studies have concentrated on which specific aspects of language are affected by brain lesions. This includes the work of Daniele et al. (1994), who documented case studies that indicated differential lexical impairment of nouns and verbs according to different sites of brain lesions. At the experimental stage their research suggested that the neural systems situated in the temporal lobe of the dominant hemisphere may be crucial to the lexical mechanisms involved in the production and comprehension of nouns. In contrast, PET scan studies have supported the critical role of the neural systems in the posterior regions of the frontal lobe in the production and comprehension of verbs. In both cases, other brain regions may also be involved in a subordinate role. Such studies do highlight the complexity of the mechanisms and demonstrate that in many instances altered vocabulary or adapted task demands may yield different results. The view of a simple serial processing of language is therefore challenged and can be examined further.

The serial or sequential processing debate

Recent research evidence challenges the traditionally held view of reading as a serial process wherein visual stimuli are converted to auditory codes. The complexity of the process can be demonstrated with reference to studies of changes in regional blood flow during single-word processing. The findings illuminated the debate on whether the processing of words is sequential, via first the visual and then the auditory pathway, or in parallel, with both occurring simultaneously. The clinical neurological literature largely supports the idea of serial processing, with visual stimuli being converted to an auditory-based code which is then used to access both the semantic and articulatory elements. In contrast, the cognitive model of word processing considers words perceived both visually and auditorally to share access in parallel to both semantic (meaning) and articulatory (pronunciation) codes. The results from the previously quoted study by Petersen et al. (1988) supported the parallel model of the separate processing of both visual and auditory access, with each having independent access to articulatory and semantic systems. Findings here indicated that no areas were activated for both auditory and visual presentation. The semantic processing of single words was found to activate frontal areas only.

For the visual modality the main activation is in the striate cortex. (The striate cortex is considered to be the primary visual cortex and is the site where visual impressions are relayed.) Evidence for this came from lesion studies that linked lesions near these areas with pure alexia (inability to read). It was considered that regions of the occipital or visual cortex might represent a network of codes involving both single letters and the more complex orthographic patterns of common visual letter strings. The activation of multiple areas could represent different levels of this network depending on the material read.

For the auditory modality, results showed bilateral activation. This was in the primary auditory cortex. An interesting finding was that certain areas were found to respond differently to words rather than to environmental sounds. This supports the idea of an initial processing into language versus non-language and a specific processing of language as opposed to more general environmental sounds. The conceptual relationships between words and sounds were studied through the medium of ERP studies by Van Patten and Rheinfelder (1995). This supported the differential hemispheric involvement in the processing of word meanings as opposed to environmental sounds. A conclusion was that non-linguistic sounds are processed differently.

An interesting finding from lesion studies has been the possible identification of one region that indicated evidence of a phonological deficit. This has been considered by some to be a potential candidate for a specific phonological coding area and is located in the temperoparietal region.

When association tasks were performed, in which subjects were required to perform certain tasks under timed conditions, there was found to be activation of two areas of the cerebral cortex for both auditory and visual presentation. Certain region-specific effects were noted. It was found that the left inferior frontal area almost certainly participates in processing semantic or meaning associations. Other specific effects were that left frontal lesions produced deficits in word-finding tests and tests of semantic priming. An area in the anterior cingulate gyrus was activated only when target selection was frequent. This was thought to indicate a region linked to attention, which was activated only when stimuli were presented in rapid succession.

Further illumination from research evidence is that certain tasks demonstrate bilateral involvement of the hemispheres in the reading process. There has recently been evidence to suggest the right hemisphere may possess the capacity to read. This premiss is in contrast to the early studies of Wernicke and was the basis of the neurolinguistic model advocated by Geschwind (1974, 1984). This model documents the significant contribution of certain right hemisphere regions and may indicate that there is bilateral involvement in the reading process and that successful reading may require the involvement of both hemispheres. This is important in the development of a neuropsychological theory of dyslexia.

The right hemisphere reading hypothesis

This challenges the idea of a left hemisphere specialization for language. Instead it proposes differential involvement according to word features. There would be a right hemisphere lexical-semantic system primarily for high imageable words. Nouns would be processed more effectively than function words such as 'and' and 'the'. Coslett and Monsul (1994), in a single case study using transcranial magnetic stimulation, found no evidence of disturbance of function when the left hemisphere was stimulated. They considered that their results could indicate that the left hemisphere might support multiple reading procedures. In contrast, the right hemisphere may support only a single semantically or meaning-mediated reading procedure. They concluded that the right hemisphere might be less capable of dealing with complex material than the left, which mediates reading for most individuals.

Advances in technology led to the possibility of more in-depth analysis of the reading process. These included PET studies, which revealed bilateral and equal central-posterior activation during the reading of words and text in both normal and dyslexic subjects. The principal difference of the studies by Hynd et al. (1987) to the earlier studies was the use of both word and text reading versus semantic recall tasks. Results were conflicting, but may again reinforce the involvement of different brain regions according to the task demands. The reading of narrative text revealed more bilateral involvement than semantic recall tasks and it was proposed that semantic recall might not activate the multiple processes involved in the complex process of reading narrative text. Hynd et al. consider that narrative text reading better represents the broad spectrum of processes involved in reading. These would include sound and word analysis, semantics, syntactics and pragmatics along with emotional and imagery aspects found in visual reading tasks. When the complexity of the reading process is considered, this argument is persuasive.

Even if the bilateral involvement in reading is accepted, that is not to say the role of each hemisphere is equal. Current theory suggests the right hemisphere is important more for the simpler language functions of naming and prosody (variation in stress, pitch and rhythm of language which convey meaning) but is still tied to and activated by a left hemisphere language system. The study by Hynd et al. demonstrated the importance of altering the nature of the reading task to obtain a more accurate picture of the bihemispheric involvement in the reading process. Evidence here was provided by examining the reading behaviour of normal subjects, but evidence can also be found by examining the behaviour of contrast groups such as dyslexic and non-dyslexic subjects.

Such analysis may reveal the differences in function between the groups when the task demands are altered. Research findings show that the right hemisphere clearly contributes to language comprehension. Part of the evidence comes from brain lesion studies which found that individuals with right hemisphere damage might have subtle language deficits such as difficulty in comprehending figurative language and making and altering inferences. In certain patients, the isolated right hemisphere can recognize words and comprehend many semantic relations, demonstrating the potential for involvement in the reading process. Mohr et al. (1994) write of a neurobiological model of lexical processing, as the neurons of the cortex are frequently active together and work in concert to strengthen their connections. There are strong connections between distant areas of the cortex and this has been likened to a large associative memory. During early language acquisition the neurons in the motor system (used for articulation) and the neurons in the auditory system (involving the auditory signal after articulation) are active together and develop associations. In most right-handed individuals this would be lateralized in the left hemisphere; for example, the content word 'house' would have visual, auditory and somatosensory (in this context, touch) stimuli causing neuronal activity in both hemispheres.

The work by Mohr et al. (1994) on lexical decision after hemispheric interaction supported the findings that the right hemisphere in concert with the left hemisphere plays a crucial role, particularly when processing content words. They concluded that direct lexical access could take place in both hemispheres. There was also support for the processing of function words in the left hemisphere. Familiarity of vocabulary was found to be a significant factor. If words are more familiar and have strong positive connections within an assembly, the whole neuron population ignites easily and quickly after stimulation. This allows for fast and accurate lexical decision. In contrast, the neuronal counterparts of non-words have weak internal connections: activity spreads more slowly with no explosive activation or ignition. In addition to word property, word frequency has also been found to reveal differences. Differential ERP response is also seen when words are categorized according to the frequency of occurrence. The work of Rugg et al. (1995) found that low frequency words had a surprising memory advantage. They concluded that this was due to memory traces representing unfamiliar events being more distinctive than the traces of less novel events.

Ongoing lateralization research with neurologically normal subjects suggests that though both hemispheres have the ability to recognize and access meaning for some words, they do not necessarily work in the same way. Experimental work has shown that differences in the extent of hemisphere activation appear to depend on the type of relations between information. Meaning activation was found to be narrower in the left hemisphere than in the right. Differences are also found in processing the emotional components of language, as several studies have found the right hemisphere to be differentially specialized for processing emotional information. Certain brain regions are the subject of ongoing research into differential function for both dyslexic and non-dyslexic populations and these include the planum temporale, the frontal lobes and the insula, and the cerebellum.

The role of the planum temporale

Evidence demonstrating the wide research interest in the functional significance of the planum temporale (Figure 1.8) can be found throughout the literature. The planum temporale is an important anatomical structure for language as it serves as the foundation for the auditory association cortex and is part of the classical Wernicke's area. It is implicated in the previously discussed Wernicke–Geschwind model of serial processing. This model received much support from neurological and neurolinguistic studies of central aphasias but has now been criticized by Kolb and Whishaw (1996) as being over-simplistic.

Within the literature there is still support for the idea that Wernicke's area includes the planum temporale and is the site for rapid whole word comprehension and that it comprises in part the auditory comprehension centre. This is supported by the findings of cytoarchitectonic (concerning the organization, structure and distribution of cells) research, which indicates the importance of the planum temporale to language. This is important as it confirms the association of anatomical differences with functional differences and has led to research into not only the function of the planum temporale but also to the study of dimension and physical features. Many have considered the identified differences in structure and size of the planum temporale (including Geschwind and Galaburda, who have developed a theory of reversed asymmetry in relation to dyslexia, i.e. that the right hemisphere is larger as opposed to the more usual pattern of the left hemisphere being larger). This begins with a developmental pattern whereby the growth of such areas as the planum temporale in the left hemisphere is delayed by testosterone. In this model the faster-growing system dominates the slower and makes more synaptic connections (synapses being the point of contact between the cells). The result of this is a larger right hemisphere with extensive network connections.

Testosterone is important in this process and can illuminate why there are more left-handed males within the dyslexic population. Theory here states that disturbed neuronal migration, especially in the left hemisphere, and the immune deficiencies found are both the results of increased levels of fetal testosterone. Galaburda (1989) extended this original theory, suggesting that since symmetrical plana are bigger, more neurons survived during development. The result is the larger right hemisphere (reversed asymmetry).

Hynd et al. (1990, 1991) suggested that the subjects did not differ in the size of the right planum. In reality the difference was in the left planum, indicating that this had been the one affected by the disturbed processes. In other words, both hemispheres were the same size, rather than the normal pattern of the left hemisphere being larger (usual asymmetry). This would be consistent with deficient linguistic abilities, as the complex skills involved in language (for most right-handed people) are mainly located in the left hemisphere. Others have linked brain symmetry closely to the causation of dyslexia (Leonard et al. 1993). They considered that the brain symmetry had a secondary function in the causation of dyslexia. The primary source of dyslexia were the cortical anomalies (or differences) during initial brain development, and the resulting symmetry was a secondary source. This theory has a dual basis, as they suggest that both of these elements are necessary for dyslexia. They suggest it is possible that the resulting symmetry diminishes the ability to compensate for the original cortical anomalies. This would limit the amount and type of strategies available to the individual and could shed some light on the complexity of the difficulties experienced by dyslexic subjects.

Various studies have demonstrated the existence of anatomical asymmetries at several locations in the brain of both adults and infants (e.g. Dalby et al. 1998). Some of these, especially concerning the temporal lobes, are believed to correlate with the behavioural manifestations of speech and hand preference. Rourke (1982) argues that this may invite the conclusion that the functional lateralization of speech is present even at the fetal stage of development. The observation that most human infants have a larger left than right planum temporale may indicate that within the left hemisphere is a predisposing programme to mediate linguistic functions. Whether this predisposition is inborn or emerges as a consequence of environmental stimuli is a matter of some debate.

These prenatal differences were confirmed by another recent study by Hynd et al. (1995), who found differences in both CT and MRI studies. Evidence here supported the idea that deviations in the development of the cortex (usually between the fifth and the seventh month of gestation) seem to result in differences in the bilateral frontal and left temporal lobes. The MRI studies indicated symmetry of the frontal lobes and variations in the sulci in the region of the planum temporale. Anomalies in the left and frontal cortical regions may be associated with abnormal patterns of activation during tasks of both phonologic listening and oral reading. Deviations in central neuroanatomy have also been found in the corpus callosum. This connects the regions of the cortex and is important in the transfer of information between the two hemispheres. There are again developmental implications, as complete myelination (the process by which the support cells of the nervous system surround and insulate axons and which is sometimes used as an index of maturation) of the corpus callosum is not achieved until late childhood and early adulthood.

The corpus callosum is also implicated in other developmental disorders such as Down's syndrome and aphasia. For dyslexic subjects the significant difference was in the size of the genu (bulbous part) of the corpus callosum (see Figure 1.11). In dyslexic subjects this was smaller than in control subjects. A moderate correlation was found between reading achievement and the relative size of the genu. Successful reading was associated with a large corpus callosum, particularly in the posterior and anterior regions. Thus there is some agreement between the behavioural and the cognitive deficit, which may be related to a defect in the transfer of information between the hemispheres – a function undertaken by the corpus callosum.

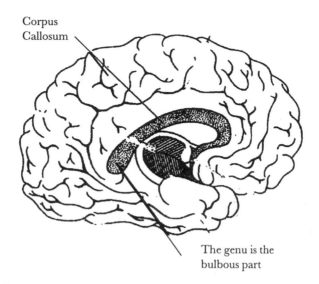

Corpus
Callosum

The genu is the
bulbous part

Figure 1.11 The Corpus Callosum and the Genu.

The populations of studies in this area vary, making it problematic to evaluate how much the results and implications of one study can generalize to different groups. This point is highlighted by Schultz et al. (1994), whose findings indicated that sex, age and overall brain size significantly affected specific areas of the brain, especially of the planum temporale. They considered this would make it difficult to find consistent results across studies. Their results emphasized this point, as when all the variables of sex, age and overall brain size were taken into consideration there were no significant neuroanatomical differences between dyslexic and normal subjects. In certain cases, however, neuroanatomical differences are great and can yield valuable data on impairment of specific function according to the site of brain lesions. Again questions need to be answered by further investigation.

When most studies on the impact of symmetrical plana are considered, the two most conclusive findings are that symmetrical or rightward asymmetry (the right hemisphere larger than the left) is associated first with poor verbal comprehension and second with poor phonological decoding. There may also be impact on expressive language skills (Morgan and Hynd 1998). Another associated difficulty may be in automatic naming ability, which again suggests an association with expressive language skills. Hynd et al. (1991) conclude there is a need to determine whether the relationship between symmetry/asymmetry and linguistic ability is revealed only in dyslexic subjects or whether similar effects can be found among non-dyslexic subjects. There is also a need to determine whether within-hemisphere or between-hemisphere differences hold the greater functional significance and to determine which particular dimensions of symmetry (length or area) are most associated with differences in linguistic ability. Research into planum temporale functions and dyslexia may ultimately add to the knowledge of the complex relationships between brain structures and behaviour. This is also being studied in relation to the insula region, which is also found in the fold within Broca's area.

Inter-modal integration: the frontal lobes and the role of the insula

It has already been shown that connections between structures are frequently implicated in the study of dyslexia. This is apparent when the complex functions of the frontal lobes are considered. The frontal lobes are generally thought to be linked to behavioural spontaneity and executive functions. Again asymmetry is a feature. The right frontal lobe is associated with such diverse elements as spatial functions relating to block design or copying and facial expression. In contrast the left frontal lobe contributes to language-related movements, such as speech (see Figure 1.12).

There is evidence from several sources that the frontal lobes are significantly involved in the processes related to reading. According to Hynd et al. (1995) these include sustained attention, regulating emotional tone, maze learning, conceptual

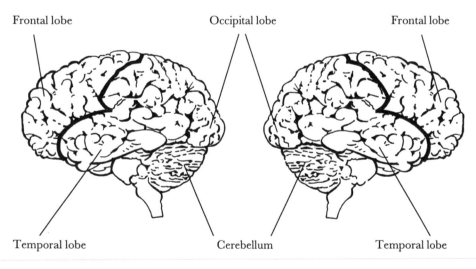

Frontal lobe   Occipital lobe   Frontal lobe

Temporal lobe   Cerebellum   Temporal lobe

Frontal lobe
in the left hemisphere involved in
language related movements
such as speech
(Also planning and reality testing)

Frontal lobe
in the right hemisphere involved in
block design or copying
(Also facial expression)

Figure 1.12 The functions of the frontal lobes.

set shifting and strategic planning. These are all higher order cognitive processes. There is also impact on the affective components of language, as the frontal lobes contain Broca's area and may be seen as central to verbal fluency and verbal learning. The connection between this and other regions is an important strand within the literature.

The idea of dyslexia as a disconnection syndrome has the work of Wernicke in 1874 as a forerunner and has been pursued by others (Birch and Belmont 1964; Geschwind 1965; Horwitz et al. 1998). Work here centred on cross-modal integration and the link between mapping heard sounds on to the visual representations of the letters and subsequently articulating them successfully. It was considered that this area may be closely involved in phonological processing. Many studies have linked a phonological deficit with anomalies in the perisylvian region, and a study by Rumsey et al. (1992) using PET scans showed differential activation patterns in the region of the angular gyrus in the left hemisphere during rhyming tasks. The dyslexic subjects also showed significantly increased activation in one right temporal region, a region which revealed no activation in the non-dyslexic control group. A main finding was that while dyslexic subjects were engaged in tasks involving phonological processing they activated the same brain area as control subjects but did not activate them in concert. More recent studies have also revealed relative under-activation in the posterior brain regions in the vicinity of the angular gyrus and relative over-activation in frontal regions (Shaywitz et al. 1998; Horwitz et al. 1998). They concluded that this pattern might provide a neural signature for the phonological difficulties characterizing dyslexia.

A group studying the role of the insula reported similar findings. Paulesu et al. (1996) recently carried out research into the differences between dyslexic and control subjects. The work again centred on the left perisylvian area of the cerebral cortex, which includes the areas of both Broca and Wernicke. The interesting conclusion of this work is regarding the role of the insula cortex in this process, as it is suggested this forms a bridge between the language areas. Evidence for this comes from PET scans on dyslexic and non-dyslexic groups. In the non-dyslexic groups, simultaneous activation was seen in each language area and the insula. In the group of dyslexic subjects, there was no apparent activation in the insula and both language areas were activated in isolation. Paulesu et al. proposed that each language area deals with a certain aspect of word processing (Wernicke for recognition of written words and Broca for the segmentation leading to a mental image of the sound of the word). The insula synchronizes the process. They suggested that normally words are processed visually and 'heard' both simultaneously and unconsciously but for the dyslexic subjects this process requires conscious effort to translate from one form to another. In non-dyslexic subjects the insula could act as a bridge between the hemispheres. In some ways this could depend on the structure of the language, as a phonological language such as English, which involves segmentation, will always require the involvement of the insula. (In languages such as Japanese, where each symbol represents a whole word, this is not necessary.) An example of the differential involvement was found in Broca's area. This was extensively activated in a rhyme decision task involving two letters but was only weakly activated in a recall task. Wernicke's area had clearly been activated during the memory task but not during the rhyming task. One important area, the insula, was not activated by the dyslexic subjects for either task. The control subjects demonstrated activation for both tasks. A surprising result was that dyslexic subjects could achieve the same performance level as the control group while using only a subset of brain area. Since the dyslexic subjects could perform the tasks it was assumed the brain areas not activated were not really necessary. Conversely, the control subjects were activating areas not required for the task. This was demonstrated experimentally when normal subjects were required to detect all descending letters in a visually presented text. Activation was found in the left perisylvian region (auditory input processing) in addition to the areas required for the visual analysis. A conclusion of this study was that dyslexic subjects could activate Broca's area for segmented phonology and Wernicke's area but they did not activate them in concert. Some areas were consistently activated to a lesser extent than were the control subjects. These were the insula, supplementary motor area (SMA) and the premotor cortex (see Figure 1.13).

Results for the insula reached a high level of significance. One observed task was to move directly from the written form of the word to associated phonology in segmented words. This task is heavily dependent on inner language and physiologically depends on the interaction between Broca's area and the supramarginal gyrus. In normal subjects both of these areas are activated along with the insula. This pattern of activation was not found in the dyslexic subjects and it was

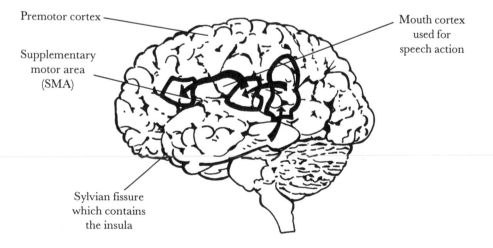

Figure 1.13 The insula, supplementary motor area (SMA) and the premotor cortex.

proposed that the insula might provide a bridge for the two areas, the function being to convert codes from one modality to another (Paulesu et al. 1996). This substantiates the earlier suggestion of Mesulam and Mufson (1985) that the insula provided for low-level integration between signals from different modalities. This is consistent with knowledge of the anatomical connections between the anterior and the posterior language areas. The lack of activation in the dyslexic subjects could indicate disconnection between the anterior and posterior speech areas, which could both impact on the performance of certain tasks.

There are clearly differences between the performance of dyslexic and non-dyslexic subjects, which may stress the importance of disconnection within the study of dyslexia. This could account for poor performance on the more demanding phonological tasks, e.g. creating Spoonerisms, for example 'car park' to 'par cark'. This is a complex skill, which requires segments of verbal material to be held in working memory. It also requires both segmented (sounds) and non-segmented codes (words) to be operated simultaneously. The dyslexic subjects exhibited isolated activation of Broca, Wernicke and the supramarginal gyrus during various phonological tasks. Paulesu et al. argued that the extent of the difficulty will depend on the degree of connectivity between the respective language areas. Weak connectivity will cause delay in establishing different language codes but would certainly impact on the learning of an alphabetic code, which depends on both correct and redundant mappings between graphemes, phonemes and the spelling of sounds and whole words. This has obvious implications for the acquisition of reading and spelling.

Support for the important contribution of the insula can also be found in lesion and brain morphology studies. It was found that lesions of the left insula could cause conduct aphasia. This is the inability to translate heard, written or self-generated words into phonemic or sound sequences. The current thinking therefore stresses the role of the left insula in having a major role in linking the various phonological codes.

Brain morphology studies have also implicated the region of the insula. Hynd et al. (1991) found significant interaction between anterior width measurements and passage comprehension. Dyslexic subjects with smaller anterior regions showed significantly poorer performance than subjects with normal asymmetry (left hemisphere larger than the right). Similarly, differences were also found in the frontal regions. Results suggested that dyslexic subjects might have insufficient substrata available for processing. Again the results demonstrated different effects for different tasks as comprehension was unaffected by reverse asymmetry.

One consistent difference that emerged demonstrated morphological differences in dyslexic subjects both in the length of the insula region and the left planum temporale. These effects were linked to deficient performance in both reading and naming tasks. In dyslexic subjects it was unclear whether poor neurolinguistic development was due to diminished regional size or again to reversed asymmetry. It is possible that a combination of factors may be necessary to create a complex syndrome such as dyslexia. Increased knowledge may reveal that the extent of the symmetry or asymmetry rather than the existence of one element such as reversed asymmetry may be necessary. Asymmetry alone may have little impact on reading performance but if found in conjunction with other effects may impact severely on performance for certain tasks. The research evidence from studies of the planum temporale and insula regions contributes to neuropsychological theory but other studies have concentrated on the involvement of the cerebellum in dyslexia.

The contribution of the cerebellum

It has been suggested that the cerebellum, in addition to contributing to motor behaviour, may also contribute to higher-level cognitive activity, including linguistic processing (Schatz et al. 1998; Rae et al. 1998). The work of Nicholson and Fawcett (1994) and Fawcett et al. (1996) has also reported high correlation between dyslexia in children and impairments in the cerebellum (see Figure 1.14).

An interesting aspect of this work is that it may lead to early detection of dyslexia in children as young as 5 years. This would be an important contribution to the field. Currently diagnosis is often made on the basis of discrepancies between reading and spelling age and chronological age, which makes early identification and intervention almost impossible. The theory of this research is that, in addition to the known involvement in motor control, the cerebellum is also implicated in language and other cognitive abilities (Fawcett et al. 1996). A simple diagnostic task involves the child standing with the arms held in front with the hands dangling limply. The angle of the hand and wrist is measured on both the

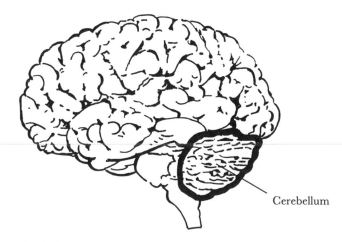

Cerebellum

Figure 1.14 The Cerebellum.

right and left sides and the difference compared. Results with dyslexic subjects have shown consistent differences of about 10 degrees. When results are compared for both normal children and slow learners there is little difference. This is important, as it may provide a solution to the difficulty of differentiating between dyslexic and slow learners, who may require qualitatively different teaching methods. Galaburda confirmed that his bank of brains of dyslexic subjects provides preliminary evidence implicating the cerebellum in dyslexia. Further empirical work by Nicholson and Fawcett (1994) revealed that for their dyslexic subjects the main defects were in reading, spelling and phonological skill and also in blindfold balance. They postulated the existence of a 'dyslexic cerebellar deficit' and replication studies showed cerebellar lesions were also linked to deficits in time estimation of dyslexic subjects.

In support of their theory they had carried out further tests. Results here had established cerebellar tests as being very sensitive to dyslexia, with two simple tests correctly classifying 90% of subjects. This measure has since been incorporated into screening tests for dyslexia, which have recently been developed for all ages and which are subject to ongoing evaluation (Fawcett and Nicholson 1996; Nicholson et al. 1998; Fawcett and Nicholson 1998b). The screening measures are the Dyslexia Early Screening Test (DEST) (Fawcett and Nicholson 1995), the Dyslexia Screening Test (DST) (Fawcett and Nicholson 1996) and the Dyslexia Adult Screening Test (DAST) (Fawcett and Nicholson 1998a). They are designed to be used by 'lightly trained professionals', so provide a welcome addition to specialist assessment materials in the dyslexia field. All provide a battery of assessments so that pupil/student profiles can be produced which can subsequently inform teaching decisions.

Studies in basic neuroprocessing

Tallal (1997) and Tallal et al. (1996) have carried out research into the theory that dyslexia may be a basic neuroprocessing problem. This concerns the inability to process sensory information rapidly, that is in the millisecond range. The factor of speed of processing was also reported by Holmes (1994), who suggested that people with dyslexia may be anatomically less well equipped to recognize speech sounds quickly. Research here centred on one of the regions that handles auditory input.

Again physiological differences were found in cell size. In dyslexic subjects the cells in this area of the left hemisphere (normally dominant for language) tend to be smaller than in either hemisphere in normal subjects. This is significant, as larger brain cells conduct signals more rapidly. The difference suggests that dyslexic subjects are slower in processing the actual sounds that constitute speech. Part of the experimental evidence centred on a decision as to which of two sounds was higher in pitch. If sounds were separated by at least 100 milliseconds, discrimination was possible, but this ability was impaired if the second sound followed the first too quickly. When processing phonetically similar sounds, for example 'b' and 'd', the difference lasts for only 40 milliseconds, so this is a serious disadvantage. During the process of reading the fine difference between these sounds is of vital importance. Developmentally, speech may be acquired more slowly during early childhood and compensation derived from metalinguistic elements such as syntax. This is insufficient when faced with reading an alphabetic language, which requires phonemic competence. Galaburda considers that this does not indicate what causes dyslexia but may rather be a secondary effect of a deeper cause. Here there would be differences between the theoretical stances of Galaburda and Tallal. Galaburda suggested that damage to the cerebral cortex early in development may cause all the other brain differences (Galaburda 1989). Tallal's work stresses the previously mentioned defect in the speed of information processing ability, and utilizes differences in speed as the factor of interest. Other workers have focused on the significance of the morphological differences in the size of various elements.

In studies using MRI techniques, Willerman (1991) found size differences in the levels of the cortex devoted to the higher mental processes of language, association and visual spatial abilities. Willerman suggested that a bigger brain means more neurons in the cortex and that the neuronal axons have more myelin sheathing. This is important, as myelin is a substance which forms an insulating layer around nerve fibres. This was supported by the work of Schulz et al. (1994), who demonstrated that more able subjects show more delineated white matter, thus indicating the increased levels of myelin sheathing which is associated with more efficient neural connections.

The time required to process stimuli has also been researched by Livingstone et al. (1991) at Harvard and was reported by Rennie in 1991. Unlike the work of Tallal, which concerned the processing of auditory information, work here centred on the processing of visual information. Studies suggested that an underlying problem of dyslexia might be the inability to perceive or distinguish rapidly changing visual stimuli (Lovegrove 1996). Research centred on the visual system, and specifically on the respective functions of the magnocellular pathway and the parvocellular pathway. (These systems exist in parallel and are responsible for transmitting information from the eyes to the visual cortex. They are named as 'magno' means large and 'parvo' small and refer to the size of the neurons making up the two systems.) The magnocellular system consists of large cells, which can respond to fast-moving, low contrast images. In contrast the parvocellular system consists of smaller cells that are sensitive to colour and fine spatial detail. Each of these systems is stimulated at different times in the reading process.

The brain activity of dyslexic subjects has been monitored by various groups and results have consistently revealed that the magnocellular pathway responded poorly to rapidly oscillating black and white patterns (Slaghuis and Pinkus 1993;

Talcott et al. 1997; Boden and Brodeur 1999). Autopsy studies revealed differences in the magnocellular pathway in that the cells were unusually small. This affected conduction, as thinner neurons conduct signals more slowly. These differences may cause information from the magnocellular and the parvocellular systems to arrive at the higher brain centres out of sequence. When performing a perceptually complex task such as reading, this mistiming may be important. This work was supported by EEG studies on disabled readers, who demonstrated long time intervals when stimuli changed rapidly (Lehmkuhle et al. 1993). Lehmkuhle et al. also confirmed the smaller magnocellular cells found by Livingstone and again linked the deficit to the temporal characteristic of the magnocellular pathway response.

Other workers question the theoretical basis of the magnocellular deficit theory as they argue that it is actually the parvocellular which is implicated in dyslexia (Skottun and Parke 1999). An interesting extension of the theory was consideration of how stimuli could possibly be manipulated to compensate for this temporal deficiency. If indeed the defect in the magnocellular pathway creates a timing disorder that interfers with the rapid and smooth integration of detailed visual information necessary for efficient reading, then there is the possibility of intervention being devised in compensation. On this issue Greatrex and Drasdo (1998) warn of the importance of clarification of the theory on the absence or existence of deficits before any intervention methods can be introduced. Once it is clear whether the deficit is in the magnocellular or the parvocellular system it may even be possible to devise screening methods to identify young children who are at risk of subsequent identification for dyslexia.

Livingstone also considered if work from the visual pathway could mirror that of the auditory pathway, which may also contain fast and slow systems. This would impact on speech perception and has certain links with the previously discussed work of Tallal. Other studies into difficulties in both the visual and auditory modalities were carried out by Eden et al. (1996), who concluded that the deficits in visuospatial function made it unlikely that reading disability could be attributed solely to left-hemisphere dysfunction resulting in phonological impairment.

Further study by Stein and Walsh (1997) concluded that the difficulties reported by many dyslexic subjects, of letters appearing to blur and move around while reading, are not the result of damage to a single visual relay system. Instead they arise from the previously reported abnormalities in the magnocellular component of the visual system, which is specialized for processing fast temporal information. The magnocellular (m-) stream culminates in the posterior parietal cortex, which is important in guiding visual attention. The result is impairment in processing fast-incoming stimuli in any of the domains of phonology, vision or movement. This would support the previously discussed work of Nicholson and Fawcett on both timing and cerebellar (equilibrium tasks) being implicated in dyslexia. Thus not just one but three domains are implicated in dyslexia, which again could help to explain the diverse difficulties experienced by dyslexic subjects.

Hormone and gender differences and dyslexia

The extensive literature on morphological studies of brain regions has been extensively discussed but other research has concentrated on both differences in hormone levels and gender differences. Although these will be reported only briefly, they are useful in showing the range of current work being undertaken in this area.

Hormone differences

Changes in neuronal growth have implications for early development and these may be affected by hormone levels. Bjargen et al. (1987) studied hormone differences between dyslexic subjects and control subjects on various hormones, including human growth hormone (HGH, which is believed to be associated with neural growth), and showed dramatic differences between the two groups. The traditional belief is that neural structures and networks are sensitive to irregularities in the developmental period and that certain systems in the central nervous system are prone to early damage. This could particularly affect such hormone-sensitive areas as the interconnected brain regions that control language learning. Rae et al. (1998) have also completed work from the biochemical perspective which has revealed biochemical asymmetry in the cerebellum in dyslexic males .

Gender differences

Other workers have also found differences related to gender in brain morphology studies. Shaywitz et al. (1995) studied sex differences with regard to the organization of the brain for language. Their work showed that activation in the inferior frontal gyrus was left-lateralized for males but bilateral for females. Female subjects therefore devoted greater right hemisphere resources to the task. (The inferior frontal gyrus is important in phonological processing tasks.) In the extrastriate region (associated with orthographic processing) there was bilateral activation by both male and female subjects. This study is important in that it demonstrated the possibility of isolating specific components of language and relating these to distinct patterns of functional organization within the normal population. These may serve to illuminate how these differ in dyslexic subjects.

Much of the evidence presented has derived from studies of either dyslexic groups or normal populations. Many would argue against dyslexia being a homogeneous syndrome and would support the hypothesis that it is a variable syndrome with different profiles being located into various subtypes. (This will be discussed in detail in Chapter 3.) If genuine differences exist, these may reveal themselves in differential brain activity between members of both different groups and subgroups. The hypothesis of differential activity was supported by EEG studies. When EEG recordings during oral reading were examined between dyslexic subtypes and groups of slow learners, attention deficit disorder (ADD) subjects and normal readers, significant differences were found. Results of these studies strongly suggested that the brains of poor readers do not process visually presented easy words in the same manner as adequate readers. Group differences were found and they concluded that when viewing letters and words, adequate readers exhibited greater power than poor readers in certain areas. They appeared to process verbal stimuli more actively. This supports the findings of the earlier work of Flynn et al. (1992). Their studies had centred on differential brain activity between dyslexic subtypes and normal control groups.

Their work had classified subjects according to the Boder subtypes of dysphonetic and dyseidetic (Boder 1973). The work of Boder involved analysis of the reading and spelling errors of dyslexic subjects and subsequently classifying them into three subtypes of dyslexia: dysphonetic, dyseidetic and mixed. The dysphonetic group used visual gestalts (wholes) for both reading and spelling words and were unable to use phonological analysis in reading and spelling. In contrast, the dyseidetic relied on phonology and were unable to read or spell irregular words. The mixed group had characteristics of both groups. The work revealed that the dyseidetic group differed most from the control group in the left temporal region and principally in the beta band (activity showing an alert state). The dysphonetic group differed at the right parietal and right occipital locations and again in the beta band. Flynn et al. had concluded these were 'rate-disabled readers' who showed an over-reliance on phonics and did not easily automatize recognition of words. It was interesting that compared to controls they differed even in those areas of the brain that had been presumed to possess processing strength. This could be interpreted as casting doubt on the compensation from strength hypothesis, which has been prevalent within the literature of learning disabilities. Instead of compensation from strength, Flynn and Deering's earlier work in 1989 had found increased electrical activity during reading in dyseidetic poor readers. This suggested that although they expended more effort in the reading process, they were using an inefficient system. They were also in danger of their need not being correctly recognized if assessment was carried out by single-word reading tests only. The authors concluded that they relied primarily on holistic visual-simultaneous processing for the recognition of words. This was markedly different from the performance of other groups. Non-disabled subjects read with minimal effort, whereas the dysphonetic were inclined to give up on meeting unknown words, or skip or misread words. This reading performance obviously uses much less energy than the intensive word-by-word decoding of the child who is dependent on phonemic decoding.

Conclusion

Work in this area is now extensive. It has a long history and has benefited from comprehensive study by many workers. Despite the technological advances, which have contributed to the theoretical knowledge, the link between knowledge of neuroanatomy and treatment or intervention is still nebulous. Some would argue that ethically it should remain so. If consistent anatomical differences are identified it could be questioned whether direct intervention would be either possible or desirable. This question was raised by the work of Leonard et al. (1993). They measured the degree of parietal shift to determine whether it was correlated with visuospatial ability. The findings of this and other MRI studies suggest that, eventually, evaluation and measurement of the morphological features of the brain may be a significant aid to the clinician and could lead to intervention and treatment based on individual brain morphology profiles. This could enable teaching to be targeted at the optimum channel for learning, and thus enable the dyslexic population to benefit from the extensive theoretical work carried out in this field. Carter (1998) writes that the discovery of a physiological sign for dyslexia may make the condition easier to recognize. Currently brain scans are clearly not an option for diagnosis, though they may lead to functional tests, which highlight central difficulties more effectively than the traditional tests of reading and spelling. There is also the (as yet) remote possibility of providing intervention, for example using a tiny 'artificial bridge' to link the relative parts of the brain which are not acting collaboratively. These possibilities seem remote but there is clearly more practical benefit to be derived from the extensive ongoing work in the field. An example of the link between theory and practice is the work of Nicholson and Fawcett (1994, 1998a) deriving from the theoretical work on the cerebellum. This has made a significant contribution to practice by the development of screening measures, which are readily available to 'lightly trained professionals' working in the field. The work of Tallal (1997) on the speed of auditory information processing also has practical implications through the development of programmes to slow down the rate of presentation of the speech sounds artificially. This work may also show the practical benefits to be derived from theoretical beginnings. The current work on the magnocellular and parvocellular pathways is currently investigating how the substantial theory can inform either assessment or intervention practice. This extension of theory to practice has already been carried out with regard to the neuropsychological theory of dyslexia. This provides another example of a useful link between theory and practice and is the substance of Chapter 2.

Chapter 2
The theoretical background

Introduction

The previous chapter documented the evidence for neurophysiological differences in dyslexic subjects. These impact on performance on certain tasks. Neuropsychological theory is based on the premiss that if the neuropsychological involvement of the brain in the reading process can be demonstrated, then a central assumption is that neuropsychological theory can be explored as a medium of improving intervention for pupils with developmental dyslexia (DD). The theory is derived from the classic animal experiments of the 1970s. The findings from animal studies demonstrate that psychological stimulation of the brain impacts not only on behaviour but also on brain parameters.

This work was reviewed in detail by Renner and Rosenzweig (1987), and showed that the brain responds differentially to enriched and impoverished environments. Evidence from this work revealed that, when brain parameters were compared between three groups of rats, there were appreciable differences according to the environmental conditions in which they had been reared. One group was raised in a standard environment, one in an impoverished environment and one in an enriched environment. The enriched environment consisted of a larger cage with play materials renewed daily. Substantial differences were found on several measures of brain parameters. These included, among others, brain weight, total amount of protein, thickness of cortex and the amount of certain chemical compounds in the cells. Several studies reported that relatively brief experience (two hours daily) in enriched environments could produce effects comparable to 24 hours per day enrichment.

Renner and Rosenzweig also cite the work of Greenough and Juraska (1979), who studied single neurons and found that the rats raised in the enriched environment had richer dendritic growth and longer dendrites (extensions of the cell body that increase the surface area and are specialized to receive information from other cells). An important feature of dendrites is the ability to grow and change throughout the life of an animal. Kolb and Whishaw (1996) write that the growth

33

of dendrites allows more connections with other neurons. These connections may be the basis for learning. Contrary to the previously held belief, it is now suggested that people who remain intellectually active have longer dendrites in old age. In contrast, diseases that produce mental retardation or senility are associated with reduced dendritic length and a reduction in the number of spines from each dendrite. Renner and Rosenzweig propose that the differing results of studies that have varied the environment may help to illuminate the complex brain-behaviour relationship. Similar conclusions were reached by Eisenberg (1995) who wrote that the mind/brain responds to both biological and social factors and is affected by both. Other experimental support is reported by Posner (1993), who found that the neural systems used for a given task could change after only 15 minutes' practice. He considered this provides evidence of the link between the structure of an organism and its experiences.

Bakker (1994) wrote of the accumulating evidence that neural parameters are responsive to environmental manipulation: the brain can therefore respond to external stimulation and may have the ability to alter its own neural structure in response to environmental influence. In an educational context, this may suggest that increased stimulation may result in actual modification of the central nervous system. This has been pursued by work with trauma cases, which has demonstrated enhanced recovery after enriched experience over a limited time.

This is also the premiss of other workers. Tallal (1997) reported on studies that have shown differences in brain activity following stimulation. Travis (1998) reported on studies by Tallal and Merzenich which demonstrated that, following intensive training, monkeys could gradually improve their identification of fast sounds. When brain scans were analysed, they found that certain brain regions had reorganized their neural circuits. The neuroanatomy of the brain had been altered as a result of specific temporal training being undertaken by the subjects. These results can be taken to demonstrate the dynamic plasticity of the brain, plasticity being the ability of the brain to change in various ways to compensate for loss of function due to (in some cases) damage. The results also demonstrate its adaptation to external stimulation. This premise can be explored and may provide insight into potential beneficial treatment applications.

One study that has explored this subject was carried out by Small et al. (1998). This was a single case study of a woman with phonological dyslexia (a form of dyslexia in which words cannot be accessed by grapheme-phoneme (letter-sound) correspondence). In this study, investigation was carried out both before and after therapy using functional magnetic resonance imaging (fMRI). Prior to therapy the woman was a reader, who responded to words immediately using a whole-word strategy. She was unable to perform grapheme-phoneme (letter-sound) decomposition on unknown words, and accessed words via the meaning or the context. Training was based on supervised training with examples of words and non-words. This led to the ability to read unknown words by explicit grapheme-phoneme analysis, which subsequently became a significant feature of her reading. It was interesting that, in addition to the observed behavioural changes (i.e. in approach to text), there were corresponding changes in the neuroanatomy of her reading. There was now increased activity in the area of the brain thought to contribute to phonological processing, and a decreased involvement in the area thought to contribute to whole-word reading. The authors suggested that functional brain reorganization had led to the activation of circuits that are usually employed in the initial stages of phonemic analysis. This study also highlights that changes may be in specific cortical areas as a result of the stimulation provided. Such studies may be taken as validation of the neuropsychological approach to intervention and demonstrate that both behaviour and the neural structure of the brain can respond positively to environmental stimulation.

The basic premiss that the brain responds to external stimulation has been developed within neuropsychological theory to provide differential intervention for dyslexic pupils. The basis of neuropsychological intervention is that different cortical areas and the way they work together can be permanently changed as a result of environmental stimulation. Additionally, the nature of the stimulation can be adapted so that specific brain regions that are thought to be under-active are specifically targeted.

Within the context of intervention, the demands of the reading process at different stages are considered and the Balance Model of learning to read is proposed (Bakker 1990).

A developmental model of reading

When the task demands of reading are analysed, it is clear the skills required change over time and these changes can be viewed as developmental stages in reading acquisition. A useful model of literacy (both reading and spelling) development was provided by Frith in 1985. This gave a three-stage model in which the child moves from an initial logographic (visual or whole-word strategy) to an alphabetic stage, where grapheme-phoneme (letter-sound) correspondences are learned and consolidated. The final stage is the orthographic stage, which is dependent on the morphemes common to the language. (Morphemes are the smallest units of language that carry meaning.) These various phases have different implications for reading and spelling.

In the **logographic phase** the child responds to a single letter or a series of letters within a word as a whole. This could be, for example, either the letter 'M' for 'McDonalds' or the letters in the child's own name. The response corresponds to the way the child responds to other objects in his or her world, such as a bicycle or a picture. The various elements within the object are given minimal attention when compared with the attention focused on the object as a whole. At this stage the child can recognize only words within his or her known sight vocabulary. He or she does not have the knowledge of letters required to access unknown words according to grapheme-phoneme analysis. Over time, and with increased exposure to print, the child begins to learn that the individual letters (and sounds) within words have meaning and ultimately can help to decode unknown words. This developing knowledge moves the child into the alphabetic stage.

In the **alphabetic phase** the child can sound out phonically regular words such as m-a-t (mat) and c-u-p (cup) and blend or synthesize them correctly. Increased skill is also evident in spelling ability and now phonically regular words will be spelled correctly and irregular words will be represented in a more logical (or phonetic) manner. The target word will contain enough key sounds and especially consonants for the word to be recognizable (for example 'mt' for 'empty', 'nrg' for 'energy' and at a later stage 'akshun' for 'action'). Here the child is building up the word correctly and is using the increased knowledge of letters but as yet has not learned the rules and conventions of English spelling.

In the final **orthographic phase** the child learns the orthography (a standardized system for writing a particular language) of English. This will include elements such as knowledge of prefixes, suffixes and that conventional letter strings such as 'str' are common in the English language whereas others such as 'xtp' do not exist. In this phase reading is fluent and skillful, and spelling generally involves correct representations of the desired words.

Thus when the reading process is considered from a developmental perspective it seems likely that different skills and possibly different brain regions will be implicated more in certain tasks than others. The diversity of these tasks will necessitate the involvement of both cerebral hemispheres. This bilateral involvement in the reading process has been discussed from a theoretical perspective in Chapter 1 and the evidence from research has indicated differential involvement according to the task demands. This is one of the basic premises of neuropsychological intervention and takes into consideration the task demands of the reading process generally.

The role of the cerebral hemispheres in the reading process

The task demands of early reading

The early reader who is at the logographic stage responds to the visual pattern of a word and does not pay attention to the individual letters. Over time, however, the child needs to become familiar with the alphabetic symbols used within an alphabetic writing system. To become familiar with these, the early reader needs to pay attention to the surface features of shape, form and direction. These unfamiliar aspects are a challenge to readers at this stage of reading development. They need to appreciate the visual perceptual differences, such as those between the letters b and d, p and q, m and w, and n and u. The small differences of orientation are crucial to the child acquiring the correct grapheme-phoneme representations of each letter and ultimately of each word. All other objects retain their unique identity when viewed from different perspectives. A kettle is still a kettle whether the spout is facing right or left or whether it is totally inverted. Letters do not behave in this way and require both form and orientation to be correct. The right hemisphere of the brain is well suited to this purpose with the emphasis on the perceptual and directional features of the visual stimuli. Experimental evidence has shown that the right hemisphere is more specialized in extracting the relevant visual and directional features from complex visuospatial information (Bradshaw and Hicks 1977; Bentin 1981; Bradshaw and Gates 1978).

In early reading the child needs ultimately to acquire knowledge of grapheme-phoneme correspondence by regular exposure to simple vocabulary. This moves the child from the logographic to the alphabetic phase, where unknown regular words can be accessed by explicit decoding or sounding out. Reading does not remain at this stage, however, as the skilled reader, who has acquired a firm knowledge of the importance of the different letter-sound value of letters, does not process each letter initially as a visual symbol, which ultimately acquires a sound. The child needs to build up the ability to recognize word-specific characteristics by repeatedly meeting similar symbols and words. This reduces the need for phonological decoding. The importance of orientation of shape and form becomes automatic and certain whole words can be recognized by sight and can be accessed immediately. Attention can now be paid to the linguistic aspects of the text. At this point, reading has assumed the intended role as a means of communication between the writer and the reader. The individual letters and sounds now require less concentration than the semantic (meaning) and syntactic (grammar) features of the text. The skilled reader can automatically process the graphophonic elements and can concentrate on the meaning of the text. The skilled reader can adapt the reading approach to the material. If material is unfamiliar or complex there may be a return to the phonological (or explicit decoding) route as no entry is available in lexical memory. An example of this would be a layperson reading medical terminology; the approach and usually the speed of reading would be different from accessing material in a newspaper. The important element is that the skilled reader can return to these earlier strategies when the occasion demands, whereas the challenge for the novice reader is to acquire the whole range of strategies.

The task demands of advanced reading

Once the initial skills are acquired, reading can begin to focus on the linguistic aspects, and this requires greater involvement on the part of the left hemisphere. For the majority of people the left hemisphere is specialized or dominant for language (Daniele et al. 1994; Paulesu et al. 1996). There is therefore a requirement for the involvement of both hemispheres within the reading process. Fries (1963) wrote of the possibility of dual hemispheric involvement in the reading process. During the process of reading one is engaged in a language activity, which activates the left hemisphere. Initially, for the novice reader during the course of reading, letter forms are perceived, which are ordered in our culture in a left to right direction. Because of this perceptual load, reading also requires the involvement of the right hemisphere. Thus in skilful reading both hemispheres have a part to play. The Novelty Model of Goldberg and Costa (1981) would support this. This presented evidence that novel information is processed by the right hemisphere and familiar information by the left. The right hemisphere is better equipped to process novel stimuli (thereby generating new concepts and descriptive systems) and the left hemisphere in processing symbolic information (using existing systems). The right hemisphere is also more suited to processing intermodal information such as grapheme-phoneme correspondence tasks, which require use of both the visual and the auditory modalities. Studies by Rourke (1982) also support the involvement of the right hemisphere in the reading process by the initial exploration of the surface features of text. Eventually, when alphabetic symbols become more familiar, the balance of activity transfers to the left hemisphere. Silverberg et al. (1979) also provide support for this initially right hemisphere involvement in the literature on foreign language acquisition. They demonstrated different brain activation patterns for foreign languages. In studies of visual field preference (VFP, to demonstrate the involvement of the hemispheres in specific tasks) they found a left VFP for English words in native Hebrew-speaking adolescents who had just begun to study English (the left VFP demonstrates the greater involvement of the right hemisphere). When VFP was measured in a group who were more experienced in the language, a right VFP (and consequently greater left hemisphere involvement) was found. The evidence here suggests there will be stronger right hemisphere involvement depending on the novelty or complexity of the new letter symbols. Galloway (1982) suggests this is a learning-to-read effect rather than a learning-a-second-language effect. A research study evaluated the implications of this for learning both Dutch and English and this will be reported in a later section (Kappers and Dekker 1995).

Experimental evidence for the involvement of both hemispheres

Experimental evidence for this can be found in several sources and by several methods, including positron emission tomography (PET, as described in Chapter 1) and studies of cerebral blood flow (CBF). Though complex procedures, these allow differential activation by the hemispheres to be seen during the reading process. The PET scan studies of Gross-Glenn et al. (1986) demonstrated asymmetrical activation of both hemispheres during reading in both normal and dyslexic subjects. Studies on CBF by Hynd et al. (1987) showed bilateral patterns of increased regional CBF (RCBF) in subjects involved in reading narrative text. This different technique also demonstrated the involvement of both hemispheres. Further work in this area by Huettner et al. (1989) reinforced the knowledge of the functional and anatomical links between the right hemisphere and the dominant left hemisphere language centre. It is hoped that in further research by controlling the various semantic and linguistic components it may be possible to obtain a more accurate bihemispheric model of the interaction of processes involved. Other evidence can be found within the literature (Coslett 1991; Coslett and Monsul 1994). The right hemisphere not only facilitates access to text but other studies have demonstrated that it also contributes to language comprehension (Richards and Chiarello 1995; Mohr et al. 1994). Thus there is considerable evidence to support the idea of two linked hemispheres, although the nature and extent of the connections required for specific tasks is still the subject of ongoing investigation. Important in this process are the links between the various modalities, and central to reading and language are the visual and the auditory domains.

The visual aspects of reading

The visual system has a central place in being one of the main routes by which information is transmitted to the cerebral hemispheres for processing. The direct connections can be seen in Figure 2.1.

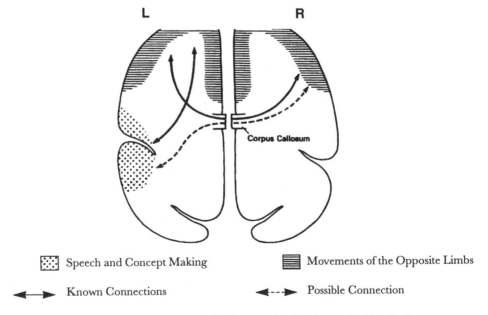

Figure 2.1 Showing how visual information is transmitted to the cerebral hemispheres.

Generally in the left of the periphery (visual field) the connections are to the right cerebral hemisphere and vice versa. The complex procedures of reading involve both of these lateral fields. Once the words are seen they need to be perceived, categorized, comprehended and articulated, thereby utilizing many brain functions. It is in these various aspects that individual differences can manifest themselves, resulting in different subtypes of learning difficulties. In the field of dyslexia there is a wide range of literature on possible subtype variation. Some would argue that the construct of subtypes is useful in that it can allow differential intervention to be devised and provided, according to individual and group differences between subjects.

The auditory aspects of reading

The auditory modality also has an important part to play in reading acquisition, as by repeated exposure to letters and their corresponding sounds the child needs to build up an accurate and consistent picture of the sounds (phonemes) associated with the different letters (graphemes). Each of the different words of the English language is composed of some of the 26 letters of the alphabet and also some of the 44 phonemes of English. As the child is learning to read, there is a need to understand that words are not just blocks of sound but are built up of different shorter sounds. Accurate reading and spelling depends on the ability to identify and manipulate these sounds successfully. The ability to carry this out is called phonemic awareness. It allows the child to carry out such tasks as rhyming, detecting non-rhymes and ultimately manipulating sound tasks such as deleting the sound 'l' from the word 'sling'. These are all measures of a child's knowledge of how the 26 letters of the alphabet combine to produce the 44 phonemes or sounds of English, and how these work together.

It is clear, when the demands of the reading process are examined, that both modalities have a part to play in taking the beginning reader successfully through the acquisition of reading competence. Many theories of reading and reading development exist, but one prevalent within the literature is the Dual Route Model of Morton (1968). Although this model represents the reading system of the skilled adult reader, it is still useful in illuminating two different approaches to reading. These are the direct or lexical route and the indirect or sublexical route.

In the direct route to reading the theory states that we recognize many words because we have encountered them so many times before that we know them. This repeated contact with the words has enabled 'logogens' (pictorial representations of the word) to be established, which include all the letters or components within the word. Once a logogen is established for a word, each time the sequence of letters within it is encountered the logogen will become active. Partial attention may be achieved for certain visually similar words, for example if there is a logogen for the word 'side', the words 'hide' and 'wide' will cause partial activation but only 'side' fulfils all the criteria. When the logogen is fired or activated a message is sent to the semantic system to retrieve the meaning of the word. The next stage is for a message to be transmitted to the pronunciation store so that the word can be pronounced accurately. In this way the direct route processes words as wholes and allows the meaning to be accessed (see Figure2.2).

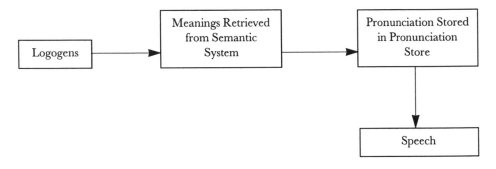

Figure 2.2 The direct route to reading.

This route is effective only when the logogens have been created, so this method cannot be used for unknown words or nonsense words. These require the indirect or sublexical route, which deals with subword units. In this process the symbols or letters are inspected visually and are mapped on to the knowledge of letter sounds and then blended to produce the correct pronunciation. It is only at this point that the meaning of the word can be accessed. Thus the indirect route cannot respond to whole words but requires first synthesis of the component parts or letters (see Figure 2.3).

Both of these models are relevant when the theory of reading, upon which neuropsychological intervention is based, is considered. This is the Balance Model of Reading (Bakker 1990).

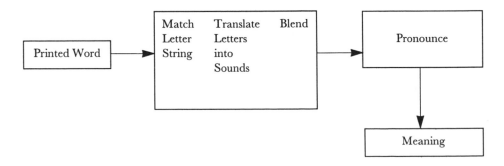
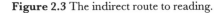

Figure 2.3 The indirect route to reading.

The Balance Model of Reading

The Balance Model of Reading considers the differential task demands of early and advanced reading where reading should be mediated primarily by the right hemisphere and then the balance of activity transfered to the left hemisphere. This is the normal developmental pattern and has been demonstrated experimentally. Licht et al. (1986) carried out studies on a sample of 74 Dutch children who were followed from kindergarten until the third grade of primary school. They found that specific changes had occurred during this time. The results of these studies found both age-related changes in hemispheric asymmetry and a changing relationship with reading ability. This was demonstrated both in repeated- and single-word reading tasks and supported the developmental change of hemispheric involvement in learning to read assumed by the Balance Model.

In certain instances this normal development does not follow the usual pattern and this is linked to the aetiology of dyslexia. Bakker (1990) has devised identification and a subtype categorization based on experimental work within the field of dyslexia and within the framework of the Balance Model.

If the expected change of hemispheric involvement in the reading process does not take place, the result can be two distinct categories of dyslexia; the linguistic (L-) type and the perceptual (P-) type. If a child begins to use the left hemisphere prematurely it may result in many inaccuracies in reading. Bakker terms these basic inaccuracies 'substantive errors' and an abundance of these characterizes the reading behaviour of the L-type dyslexic child.

The L-type dyslexic pupil attempts to read with little regard to the perceptual features of the text. Reading is fast and may demonstrate many inaccurate responses to the surface features of the text. There may be evidence of reversals such as 'on' and 'no' and 'saw' and 'was'. Other inaccuracies may show both inversions and reversals of letters within words such as 'me' and 'we' (inversion of m/w) and 'not' and "out" (inversion and reversal of position of n/u). Words or sentences may be reversed so that the meaning of the text is altered and the communication lost. Words, sentences and even whole lines of text may be omitted. This is the reader who may misread function words such as 'the' and 'that' and consequently may show a depressed accuracy score when a standardized test of reading is administered. This pattern of errors may be seen as common features of the reading of many dyslexic pupils and form a group all too recognizable by teachers of dyslexic pupils. These pupils find it difficult to assimilate the fine perceptual differences between the alphabetic symbols and attempt to access the text by global access to the meaning. This reader may also be conceptualized as reading via the direct route (see Figure 2.2).

Here, words that have previously established logogens are accessed directly by the visual/lexical route, with no recourse to phonemic decoding. The disadvantage of this method of reading is that there appears to be inadequate basic knowledge of sound/symbol correspondence, which results in fast but inaccurate reading.

The other subtype, the perceptual (P-) type pupil is equally disadvantaged but in a different way. This pupil has begun to read using the hemisphere best suited to initial reading but has subsequently failed to transfer the balance of activity involved in reading to the left hemisphere. If a child does not make the switch from predominantly right to left-mediated strategies, his or her reading is characterized by slow and fragmented reading. Bakker terms this pupil the P-type as they have failed to make the transfer to the more fluent and skilful left hemisphere reading. Reading here is characterized by slow reading which is lacking in fluency. Errors here will almost certainly impact on the rate of reading and in most cases also the fluency of the reading. Reading behaviour will be adversely affected by a reliance on spelling-like reading. Words may be sounded out according to their graphophonic properties almost on a word-by-word basis. These pupils may show an over-reliance on the physical symbol, for example the word 'had' may be overtly decoded many times on the same page despite being successfully synthesized on the first occasion. This may be seen not as a fault of either short- or long-term memory but of an approach to text. Another example would be of the pupil who attacks the regular word 'had' and the far more complex word 'television' by attempting graphophonic conversion. For this group the very skills deficient in the L-types are a weakness, as they are inappropriately over-used. Pupils within this group demonstrate use of the indirect route to reading, which relies heavily on graphophonic conversion of individual letters and sounds (see Figure 2.3).

The impact on the reading of this subtype is as severe as for the L-types as there may be greater impact on comprehension. The quality of the message between the writer and the reader must be lost in the midst of individual sound/symbol conversion of many words in the text. Recent studies have stressed the importance of the measurement of rate of reading in addition to accuracy and comprehension. Demb et al. (1998) found that slow rate of reading is one of the most sensitive markers of dyslexia in adults with a childhood history of dyslexia. Despite the existence of compensation methods in other aspects of reading, reading rate was still reduced.

The differences between the two subtypes will be discussed in greater detail, but Table 2.1 summarizes the main characteristics of the subtypes in their reading behaviour.

Here it can be seen that the slow and accurate reading behaviour exhibited by the P-type dyslexic pupils relies heavily on the alphabetic symbols, which implies increased involvement by the right hemisphere. They use the indirect route to reading and use the auditory channel while explicitly decoding words. In contrast, the L-type pupils demonstrate use of the direct or lexical route to text. They respond quickly (and often inaccurately) to whole words, which implies greater involvement of the left or linguistic hemisphere.

Table 2.1 Reading behaviour of P-types and L-types

	P-type	L-type
Preferred modality	Auditory	Visual
Reading route	Indirect	Direct
Reading behaviour	Slow/accurate	Fast/inaccurate
Balance of hemisphere activity	Right	Left

Development of intervention programmes

It is these differences which are crucial in the construction of differentiated teaching programmes to match instruction to the needs and individual learning style of the pupils. Knowledge of the subtypes of specific learning difficulties is therefore required for teaching approaches to be matched to pupil needs. Bakker has devised both classification and intervention systems based on these subtype differences (Bakker et al. 1981, 1990, 1995; Bakker and Licht, 1986; Grace 1990; Kappers 1997; Kappers and Bos 1990; Kappers and Hamburger 1994; Masutto et al. 1993, 1994; Robertson 1996, 1997, 1999). Findings between studies vary. Some studies provide more critical results (Grace and Spreen 1994). Research design can contribute to certain of the differences, such as differences in time, length and duration of treatment sessions, subject selection and classification and stability of subtype over time. All need ultimately to be resolved by further study but may provide indications of a treatment model, which may benefit certain dyslexic subjects.

Conclusion

The development of neuropsychological intervention for children with dyslexia is supported both by the theory concerning the response of the brain to stimulation, and the theory concerning the different task demands of the reading process according to the reading proficiency of the reader. This combination of research background, assessment and differentiated intervention is rare within the study of dyslexia and may ultimately lead to extension of the range of strategies that are currently available for dyslexic subjects.

Chapter 3
Allocation to subtype

The existence of subtypes

It can be argued that the Balance Model of dyslexia discussed in Chapter 2
supports the identification of different subtypes of dyslexia. Identification of the
subtypes may be made by observing directly the different reading behaviour of
pupils. Within the field of dyslexia, the existence of different subtypes is controversial. Many argue against their existence as they see the key differences between
dyslexic subjects as quantitative. If the difference is quantitative the subjects differ
only in the extent of the difficulties in a range from mild to severe (Bryant and
Goswami 1990; Stanovich 1991; Metsala et al. 1998; Stanovich et al. 1997).
Others argue that the differences are qualitative in that the observed difficulties
are substantively different from those demonstrated in pupils with more generalized reading difficulties (Boder 1973; Gjessing and Karlsen 1989; Bakker 1990,
1994, 1997; Borsting et al. 1996; Manis et al. 1996; Frith 1997).

Ultimately the argument rests on whether the differences between dyslexic
subjects are qualitative or quantitative and whether these differences can enable
differential intervention to be devised. Hooper (1996) writes of the need for a more
refined and ecologically valid diagnostic system. He presented a comprehensive
overview of the history of the study of individuals with specific learning difficulties
dating back more than 100 years. Much of the evidence derived from single case
studies such as Kussmaul (1877) and Morgan (1896) and from single-factor
theories such as Orton (1925). These contributed to the general knowledge base
on dyslexia but did not seem to account for the variety of differences observed in
the children and adolescents with learning problems. Theories began to evolve,
which hypothesized the existence of various classifications, and it was hoped these
would lead to improved identification and response to intervention. These classification approaches can be divided into clinical-inferential approaches and empirical subtyping.

The work of Boder (1973) is an example of the clinical-inferential approach
and derives from her observations on the reading and spelling errors of dyslexic

45

subjects in a clinical setting. During the course of her work with pupils who had failed to acquire basic skills of reading and spelling she observed certain common characteristics. This led to investigation into the types and patterns of reading and spelling errors made by students. She found that nearly all students who had been diagnosed as being dyslexic had one or another of three dyslexic reading-spelling patterns. This supported her theory that these three patterns reflected specific cognitive deficits and subsequently led to development of the Boder Test of Reading and Spelling Patterns (Boder and Jarrico 1982), by which the subtypes could be identified.

Empirical subtyping utilizes methods such as cluster analysis, which identifies psychoeducational, intellectual and neuropsychological variables to group individuals. These approaches require a clear operational definition of dyslexia and a classification system which provide clear guidelines on which subjects are to be assigned to the respective categories. It was expected that the identification of subtypes would enable advances to be made in aetiology and prognosis, and could become instrumental in the development of early identification and prevention techniques. All of these may eventually improve the quality of services to children in need so that differentiated intervention can be provided. Some workers believe that subtype theory may have contributed to our understanding of the range of difficulties found in dyslexia.

Subtype theory

Subtype theory allows us to examine both the differences between groups and the differences within groups. It would be naïve to write of pupils with dyslexia as representing a unitary group, and subtype theory is an attempt to examine certain prevalent characteristics. Two dimensions that have consistently been the subject of investigation have been the visual and the auditory modalities. Many references can be found within the literature (Gjessing and Karlsen 1989; Johnson and Myklebust 1967; Bateman 1968; Mattis et al. 1975; Flynn et al. 1992; Stein and Walsh 1997; Ridder et al. 1997).

Within the auditory domain, extensive research has emerged on the importance of phonological awareness to an understanding of dyslexia (Bryant et al. 1989; Bruck 1992; Gough and Tunmer 1986; Snowling 1995, 1997; Paulesu et al. 1996). Arguments here rest on the assumption that while there may be variability in the observed signs, the underlying cognitive deficit (resulting in poor grapheme-phoneme conversion and a phonological deficit) is common to all subjects (Frith 1997). Frith writes of the wealth of evidence that dyslexia has a genetic origin and of the evidence for a brain abnormality affecting the areas which subserve phonological processing (Galaburda 1989; Rumsey et al. 1992). The weakness in the phonological system leads to problems in speech processing and difficulties in learning to read and spell. These biological differences are the basis of the differences between the pupil with dyslexia and the pupil with general reading difficulties. In the case of the pupil with dyslexia, the differences are found at three levels (see Figure 3.1). These are the biological (brain abnormality), the cognitive (phonological deficit) and the behavioural (poor reading and spelling). When a poor reader is considered, differences are at two levels only: that is the cognitive and the behavioural. Thus there are two populations who may appear to share some common difficulties but who will almost certainly require different levels of support, and in some cases different types of support. For the dyslexic group, many workers believe that much of the intervention will centre on phonological assessment and training.

Workers in the field of visual processing do not subscribe to this theory. Substantial work has been carried out within the visual domain and has concentrated on a visual processing deficit (Cornelissen et al. 1995, 1997; Edwards et al. 1994; Watson and Willows 1993; Hogben 1997; Stein 1997; Talcott et al. 1997).

Work is ongoing and much research now centres on the relative differences between the magnocellular and the parvocellular systems in dyslexic subjects. These two parallel pathways both extend from the retina into the visual cortex, where they segregate into separate layers of large (magnocellular) and small (parvocellular) cells. Both systems have different properties. The magnocellular system responds to lower spatial frequency and higher temporal frequency stimulation. It responds mainly to the beginning and end of stimuli and produces responses that are typically rapid and short in duration. It does not respond to differences within shades of colour but may respond to luminance. In contrast, the parvocellular system, produces slower and more durable responses. Unlike the

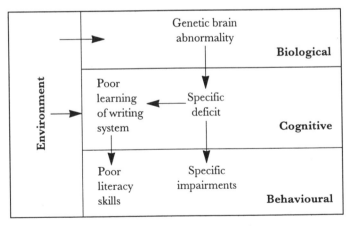

(Reproduced after Frith 1997)

Figure 3.1 Basic causal model demonstrating different levels of explanation.

magnocellular system it can distinguish between shades of a given colour range. Experimental work has demonstrated that within dyslexic subjects there is a deficit in the magnocellular system (Lovegrove et al. 1986; Galaburda and Livingstone 1993; Gross-Glenn et al. 1995; Cornelissen et al. 1995; Edwards et al. 1994; Kubova et al. 1996). Lehmkuhle et al. (1993) suggest that the magnocellular deficit creates a timing disorder that precludes the rapid and smooth integration of detailed visual information which is necessary for efficient reading. Certain workers note that this deficit may also coincide with concomitant difficulties in phonological processing but there is, as yet, little clear evidence about how the factors may relate to one another (Slaghuis et al. 1993). Other workers argue that a magnocellular deficit may be part of a more general deficit of central nervous system functioning (Livingstone et al. 1991).

The timing of responses to auditory as opposed to visual stimuli has also been the focus of some researchers (Holmes 1994; Miller and Tallal 1995; Tallal 1980, 1997; Tallal et al. 1996). Work here suggests that the deficit involves the inability to process sensory information rapidly. This affects the ability to identify fast elements embedded in ongoing speech that have durations in the range of a few tens of milliseconds. This is a critical time frame over which many phonemic contrasts are signalled, for example 'ba' and 'da', which are characterized by very rapid frequency changes that occur during the first few tens of milliseconds. An interesting finding was that when the rates of changes were synthetically extended in time about twofold, identification of the same syllables became possible. This led to the development of an intervention programme in which the critical formant transitions were emphasized and extended in time. The same children also received training in making distinctions about fast and rapidly sequenced acoustic inputs in exercises delivered by computer games. This training in the application of temporally modified speech led to an improvement in phonological discrimination in the subjects studied.

When the research evidence is examined, there does therefore seem to be at least two qualitatively different groups of subjects. Both have major implications for the type of intervention required to assist them in overcoming the observed reading and spelling difficulties. A central issue is whether the construct of subtype can usefully inform decisions on suitable intervention.

Subtype theory and relevance to teaching

Subtype theory may be considered to appeal to many teachers who feel that it has usefulness in illuminating some of the differences they observe between individuals. Experienced practitioners recognize that while individual differences certainly exist between dyslexic subjects, subtype theory may be useful in informing teaching decisions. Within an educational context teachers generally teach to strengths so that weak modality channels can be supported by stronger ones. Within the dyslexia literature two strong divisions already discussed are those of the visual and the auditory modalities and substantial reference to literature within these areas has already been made.

Subtype theory may be regarded as a medium for devising differential intervention for pupils, and here the original experimental work of Bakker (1990) led to the development of differential intervention. Bakker argues that if the needs of the different subtypes revealed by the Balance Model are examined, clear guidelines may be found for suitable intervention strategies.

These can be introduced by examining how the sub-type categories of Bakker relate to those of other workers.

Parallels between the subtypes of Bakker and other workers

Influential within subtype literature is the previously mentioned work of Boder (1973). Her work, which was derived from clinical observations, led to postulation of the existence of three main classifications of dyslexia. These were the dysphonetic (and largest group), the dyseidetic and the alexic group. The dysphonetic group were 'direct route readers', who could access text globally but who experienced great difficulties with phonemic analysis. Their approach to text was not mediated by sound/symbol correspondence and their problems can be conceptualized as being in the auditory domain. In contrast, the dyseidetic group were 'indirect route readers' who had poor memory for visual configurations and word gestalts and relied heavily on phonemic analysis in compensation. This group can be seen as having difficulties mainly in the visual modality. The alexic group had difficulties in both modalities and in effect showed some characteristics of both groups.

Clear parallels can be found between the visual and auditory subtypes already discussed and the subtypes of Bakker. The arguments are complex, however, and a straight one-to-one correspondence cannot be found (see Table 3.1).

The L-type pupil relies predominantly on the visual input channel and uses the 'direct route' approach to text. Although this is the preferred channel it is not a strength, as reliance on this channel is inappropriate. It is not only a use of the visual channel but an overuse, as the perceptual care required is not utilized. Attention is perceptually careless and the number of substantive (real) errors produced by the reading provides evidence of this. The number of these substantive errors can be quantified by formal error analysis of the reading. When the reading of the P-type pupil is scrutinized, clear differences in error performance are revealed. Here, reliance seems to be on the auditory channel and reading is via the 'indirect route'. Again, though the preferred channel, it is not a strength, as overuse renders the method inappropriate for much of the text. Attention for this group is focused on sound–symbol correspondence and evidence is found in the number of fragmentation or time-consuming errors. Teacher assessment can enable allocation to subtype and differential intervention to take place.

Table 3.1 Reading behaviour of P-types and L-types

	P-type	L-type
Preferred modality	Auditory	Visual
Reading route	Indirect	Direct
Attention focus	Perceptual	Semantics
Balance of hemisphere activity	Right	Left

Example of how pupils are assessed and allocated to groups

For classification purposes an analysis of reading errors will be made according to the criteria described by Bakker. These will be outlined briefly below. (Specific guidelines can be found in Appendix 1).

Reading material

The reading material for the pupil is a text slightly higher than the pupil's independent reading level and the basis of the approach stems from a miscue analysis model. Historically, this approach derives from the work of Goodman (1973) and Arnold (1982). Beard (1987) describes the approach as revealing a window on the reading process.

Miscue analysis is a classic approach utilized by many teachers to ascertain the complex interaction between a pupil and a text. This forms the basis of the Bakker subtype allocation procedure. The classic error categories of substitutions and omissions form the basis of the substantive error categories. The error category for the fragmentation errors extends the categorization of the standard inaccurate responses to text, to take into account those errors which impact on fluency. Here can be found reading, which relies heavily on overt grapheme–phoneme correspondence and which impacts on the time taken for the reading. In the case of certain pupils, there is also impact on reading comprehension, for if too much attention is paid to the letters as symbols the meaning of the text may be lost.

A strength of this approach is that it can use a standardized measure of text reading such as the Neale Analysis of Reading Ability (NARA) (Neale 1989) or the Macmillan Reading Analysis (Macmillan 1989). The analysis can then be extended to allow for assessment of the fragmentation errors made by the pupil to be taken into account. This may enable a more accurate description to be obtained of the reading process for particular pupils.

Allocation to subtype

It is suggested that the reading should be tape-recorded so that analysis can be checked subsequently. This also enables the test administrator to become more competent in analysing the test data, and in particular to refine diagnosis of the time-consuming errors which have been shown to be more difficult to define and identify.

After the administration of a reading test, pupils are ranked according to the number of errors of each type (substantive or fragmentation) they have made. Substantive errors include omissions, reversals, additions and word mutilations; in fact, all real errors. Fragmentation errors include all 'spelling-like' reading, hesitations and repetitions. If the child makes more than an average number of substantive errors in addition to less than an average number of time-consuming errors they are classed as an L-type dyslexic child. If the child scores below average on substantive errors and above average on fragmentation errors they are classed as being a P-type dyslexic child. Tables 3.2 and 3.3 demonstrate how the profiles of the type and number of errors are different for the L- and P-type pupil respectively. In Table 3.2, relating to pupil A, it can immediately be observed that the majority of errors are substantive errors and few fragmentation errors have been made.

Table 3.2 Example of error analysis based on pupil reading of the NARA (pupil A)

Text	Pupil response	Type of error
Bicycles	Bikes	Substantive
Had	Were	Substantive
Quickly	Quick	Substantive
Saw	Was	Substantive
Pointed	Panted	Substantive
Television	Telephone	Substantive
A	The	Substantive
Sheltered	Sh...	Fragmentation
His	Has	Substantive
Spring	Straight (self-corrected)	Substantive
	Spring	Fragmentation
Instantly	Instately	Substantive
Thrown	Threw	Substantive
An	The	Substantive
Underground	Dungeon	Substantive
With	Was (self-correction)	Substantive
	With	Fragmentation
Jewels	Jelly	Substantive
Rested	Reached	Substantive
Awhile	And while	Substantive
Desert	Desides	Substantive
Travellers	Travels	Substantive
Often	Oven	Substantive
Strange	Stage	Substantive
Palace	Place	Substantive
That	Had (self-corrected)	Substantive
	That	Fragmentation

When the errors are analysed there are 23 occasions when the pupil has made a substantive error and only four occasions when he has made fragmentation errors. When the responses are analysed there appear to be many immediate responses to the text on the basis of a superficial resemblance to one or two letters. Some are more successful than others and result in words similar to the stimulus word, whereas others are semantic substitutions (for example 'underground' for 'dungeon'). Examples such as 'jelly' for 'jewels' seem to derive from a superficial similarity to the original word. It is interesting that of the four fragmentation errors made by this pupil, three are self-corrections and seem to have been changed in accord with the meaning and the context of the passage. One other interesting aspect of this reading was that it was very fast and the motivation of the pupil was good.

The passage was at a suitable level of reading and was carried out in accord with the administration guidelines given for the particular instrument, yet many errors were noted. Some errors were occasioned by function words such as 'has' for 'his' and 'an' for 'the', which would be presumed to be familiar words to the pupil. With the exception of 'deside' and 'instately', all of the words produced by the pupil were real words. Despite the number of errors, it was surprising that the pupil was able to answer some comprehension questions (although these could not be calculated into a reading comprehension age due to the guidelines for the measure). It is also interesting that this pupil had been receiving individual support for dyslexia for two years by this time. This had been delivered by traditional multisensory methods, which have a high degree of phonic analysis, yet there had been very little impact on the pupil's preferred reading style. This can be contrasted with the results of another pupil, whose reading demonstrates a different approach to text (see Table 3.3).

When the results for this pupil are analysed, a different pattern emerges from that obtained for pupil A. In this case, the pupil made a total of 18 fragmentation errors and only 10 substantive errors. The pattern of the errors appears different in that this pupil attempts to use explicit decoding to access the words, yet does not complete this process successfully on any occasion. The reading rate of this pupil was slow (the second passage of 52 words took 182 seconds) with many hesitations and attempts at either the first letter only or the first two letters. The comprehension score for this pupil was lower than that of pupil A, although the number of inaccurate responses to the text (in terms of actual errors scored on the measurement) was fewer. On three occasions the same errors or unsuccessful attempts were repeated.

These two examples serve to highlight the different reading styles of the two pupils and demonstrate their needs in respect of successful reading acquisition. Error analysis, however, is subjective and in one study the writer carried out an inter-rater reliability on the test results of one subject. This provided, albeit limited, evidence that substantive errors are easily recognized by teachers but that the fragmentation errors are more difficult to identify. In this exercise, the author and a reading specialist independently listened to a tape-recording of a pupil being assessed with a NARA. When subsequently analysed, reliability between the two

Table 3.3 Error analysis based on pupil reading of the NARA (pupil B)

Text	Pupil response	Type of error
Nice	Nice (repetition)	Fragmentation
Lane	Line	Substantive
Their	They	Substantive
Crashed	Crushed	Substantive
Bicycles	B...b...icycles	Fragmentation
No-one	On-one	Substantive
Ali	Ail	Substantive
Sheltered	Sh...sh...sh	Fragmentation (3)
Sent	S-en-t	Fragmentation
Instantly	Inst	Fragmentation
–	Inside	Substantive
	Inside (twice)	Fragmentation (2)
Underground	Overground	Substantive
Covered	c-o-v-e-r-e-d	Fragmentation
Ali	Al (2)	Substantive
		Fragmentation (2)
Travellers	tr-a-v-els (2)	Substantive
		Fragmentation
Escape	Ess-cay-p	Fragmentation
Stones	St...	Fragmentation
Place	Pl...a...ce	Fragmentation
Built	Brought	Substantive
A long	Al...al....	Fragmentation
Time	ti-me	Fragmentation

assessors on the substantive errors was found to be 82% but for the fragmentation errors was reduced to 50%. This may be seen to demonstrate a familiar as opposed to an unfamiliar approach to the reading process, whereby if a child ultimately decodes the word accurately, the route to accuracy is unimportant. In fact, teachers generally perceive word-building skills as being a valuable addition to the reading skill of pupils. If over-utilized, however, over-reliance on word building or explicit decoding can impair fluency and access to the meaning of the text.

Another factor that can demonstrate the differences between the two subtypes is that of reading speed and in several studies this has been included in conjunction with the type of reading errors. The L-type pupil typically reads faster than the P-type pupil, and the speed of reading in conjunction with the main type of reading error is a significant difference between the two subgroups.

According to the Bakker theory, children thus classified will be designated as either L- or P-types and subsequently receive either L- or P-type intervention. This has been found to allow differential treatment effects to be noted by several workers. (This will be discussed in greater detail in subsequent chapters.)

The developmental model

In the event of a child not possessing the minimum required reading level for classification purposes, the theory proposes that the developmental model of stimulating initially the right hemisphere be followed (Kappers 1997). This would allow the child to concentrate on the initial perceptual features of the text and, following consolidation, to move to stimulation of the left (linguistic) hemisphere. The decision tree (Figure 3.2) formulated by Kappers and Hamburger (1994) can inform the choice of hemisphere for stimulation.

In the case of a non-reader, a minimum number of high frequency words (for example five or ten) would be taught so that the stimulation of the right hemisphere could commence in accord with the developmental model. This would also be supported by the previously discussed Frith model, as whole words allow the child to operate at the first stage of reading development – the logographic stage. (In the case of a non-reader, these words would usually be delivered by hemisphere-specific stimulation (HSS), which is discussed in detail later in the chapter.) If analysis of the child's reading behaviour revealed difficulties in the early stages of reading, such as letter identification and phoneme–grapheme correspondence, stimulation would also begin initially with the right hemisphere. A pupil who was reading at a more advanced level, but whose reading behaviour was fast but generally inaccurate, would also receive stimulation of the right hemisphere. In contrast, a pupil whose reading was slow with an emphasis on explicit grapheme–phoneme analysis, but usually ultimately accurate, would receive stimulation of the left hemisphere to encourage reading fluency (Licht 1994). These are in accord with the theory of reading being a developmental process wherein certain skills are more important at certain stages.

Problems of classification

A study by the author (Robertson 1996) revealed evidence of difficulties in classification, as many pupils fitted into neither category but showed the characteristics of both groups. Within the literature this difficulty is acknowledged, as Bakker (1990)

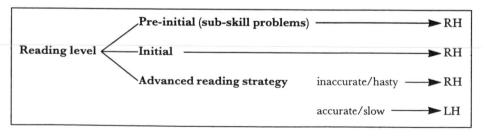

Figure 3.2 Decision tree for selection of target hemisphere.

estimates that his subtype categories account for only 60% of pupils. When the assessment results for the unclassifiable pupils were examined they seemed to form yet another subgroup. This group was designated as a mixed group (M-type) and subsequent study revealed their responses to be qualitatively different from either the L-type or the P-type subjects.

Other workers investigating the Bakker categories have since incorporated a mixed subtype into their classification system as an extension of the traditional Bakker categories (Masutto et al. 1994). The existence of a mixed subtype is again similar to the work of Boder, who included a mixed dysphonetic/dyseidetic category into her initial classification system (1973). The Masutto et al. (1994) study on Italian children included an analysis of the subtypes of both Boder and Bakker. In a group of 38 children, they found not only differences in reading errors but significant differences in a range of cognitive functions, including dichotic listening. (Dichotic listening is the procedure of simultaneously presenting a different auditory input to each ear through stereophonic headphones. Differential patterns of activation can reveal which hemisphere is most affected by the stimulus. A normal pattern of activation reveals a right ear advantage (REA, showing involvement of the left hemisphere) for verbal tasks, which reflects the greater involvement of the left hemisphere in linguistic processes.) They found that the L-type dyslexic pupils (10 subjects) showed an increased number of substantive errors, in addition to low scores in verbal short-term memory and a right ear advantage in dichotic listening. In contrast, the P-type pupils (18 subjects) showed few reading errors, a short attention span, low performance in visual-motor co-ordination (coding subtest of the Wechsler Intelligence Scale for Children-Revised (WISC-R; Wechsler 1976) and an absence of REA in dichotic listening tasks (indicating the involvement of both hemispheres). The M-type pupils (10 subjects) showed numerous reading errors, low performance in visual–motor co-ordination tasks (coding) and REA in dichotic listening. The authors speculated that the results might indicate that the left ear advantage for verbal stimuli could be a reflection of the right hemisphere being over-engaged in linguistic function. This could compromise non-verbal abilities such as visual perception and attention. They considered that the reorganization of hemisphere specialization could be an expression of left hemisphere dysfunction. This has also been the conclusion of other workers (Flynn and Deering 1989).

Such research not only demonstrates the cognitive differences between the subtypes but may also indicate how the subtype categories can be further refined and extended. This may indicate that differential intervention may be targeted even more specifically if the subtypes are extended beyond that of the two original Bakker subgroups. It may also be seen to reflect the developmental approach to the acquisition of reading competence as described by the Balance Model. If, as Bakker argues, initial reading is mediated by the right hemisphere and is dominated by perceptual care, and advanced reading is primarily mediated by the left hemisphere (emphasis on linguistic strategies), it would be simplistic to believe this transfer of activity happens overnight. While the pupil is assimilating use of the linguistic strategies there will be fluctuation according to such factors as familiarity with the text and pupil confidence with the material. This could mean that there is a period of fluctuation where differences can be revealed. In fact, even a subtype model of only three categories may be oversimplistic. Certain pupils were severe L-types and others severe P-types and certain pupils ranged between the two. In the end a continuum of dyslexia could be proposed between these two and this could inform differential intervention even more specifically.

For differential intervention to be successful, the problem of how pupils are classified must be resolved. Bakker himself emphasized this (Bakker, 1990). Studies to date have shown that pupil classification is not consistent or stable. Pupils who are classed as L-types in one study would not necessarily be L-types in another study. Variable results can be due to the measure on which subtype allocation is made. Grace and Spreen (1994) write of the difficulties of the 'and/or' clause within the literature. This refers to the L-type demonstrating REA *and/or* faster reading along with *and/or* a high proportion of substantive errors in some studies, but in other studies allocation may be made only on the basis of one of these elements.

There is also concern that the subtype may not be consistent over time. The author carried out a small-scale study in 1996 and concluded that of the 37 pupils studied, 20 remained stable over three occasions of testing but 17 showed variation (see Table 3.4). The time difference between testing was 12 weeks (between occasion 1 and occasion 2) and 16 weeks (between occasions 2 and 3).

Table 3.4 Changes in subtype over three occasions of testing

Occasion 1	Occasion 2	Occasion 3
L	M	M
L	M	M
L	L	M
L	M	P
M	L	L
P	M	P
M	M	L
L	L	M
M	L	M
L	M	L
L	M	M
L	M	M
L	L	M
L	M	P
L	M	M
P	P	M
M	M	L

When analysed, the results show that in most cases the change was in the predicted direction. That is to say, the pupils who had been L-types changed to an M-type category. They would have shown an increase in reading accuracy (and a corresponding decrease in substantive errors) and/or a decreased rate of reading. Both of the P-type pupils also changed to the M-type category (although one subsequently reverted back to the P-type category). This again shows change in the predicted direction, that is an increase in either or both reading fluency and a faster response to text.

When these results are examined, some change in subtype may have been the result of intervention being successful in the predicted direction. For example, it might be assumed that the profile of errors of an L-type pupil may change as a result of successful stimulation of the right hemisphere, which could result in a decrease in the number of substantive errors and a slower rate of reading. For example, when the results for the first three pupils are analysed, it can be seen that there is a consistent change from the L-type category to the M-type category. This demonstrates a reduction of substantive errors and an increase in fragmentation errors, which could indicate the beginnings of perceptual care towards text. There is a clear need for difficulties in initial classification to be overcome if differential intervention is to be the focus of further investigation.

The strength of the neuropsychological approach

The strength of the neuropsychological approach is that it can allow differentiated intervention to be provided for pupils on the basis of observed and measured deficits in the reading performance. These are different to traditional remedial approaches in that the target is to alter the mode of information processing. It can therefore be seen to be corrective as it aims to alter the information-processing approach of the pupil in a prescribed direction. Observed deficits are then targeted for teaching and these form the basis of the intervention. Intervention can be provided either by hemisphere-specific stimulation (HSS) or hemisphere-alluding stimulation (HAS) (see below), but both can provide differential intervention according to the subtype of the pupil and the perceived needs relative to their reading development.

Development of the programmes of intervention

Hemisphere-alluding stimulation (HAS) utilizes modified text and is differentiated to stimulate the left and right cerebral hemispheres respectively. The text is modified so that it can appeal (or allude) more to either the right hemisphere (for L-type subjects) or the left hemisphere (for P-type subjects).

Hemisphere-specific stimulation (HSS) can be provided to stimulate the theoretically deficient hemisphere directly. Stimulation can be delivered either by the tactile receptors of the hands or by haptic (visual) perception via computer. Computer-delivered HSS uses knowledge of the visual half-fields to appeal directly to either the left or the right cerebral hemisphere. In both cases, a central image ensures the subject's gaze is directed to the centre of a computer screen. The subject focuses on this fixation point and a word or a series of letters is flashed to the right or left visual half-field for a brief period of time (in a range up to 300 milliseconds only). Thus the stimulation is directed at either the left or the right cerebral hemisphere via the visual half-fields and at a rapid rate so that explicit 'reading' is not possible. HSS tactile is delivered when the pupil feels letters with the fingers of the left or right hand and thus transmits the stimulus directly to the appropriate hemisphere. In both cases, access to the letters is by touch only and the pupil has no visual access to the letters and words. In the case of an L-type pupil, letters are felt with the fingers of the left hand to stimulate the theoretically deficient right hemisphere. Conversely the P-type pupil has the material presented to the fingers of the right hand to stimulate the theoretically deficient left hemisphere. Both methods can therefore provide differentiated intervention according to the theoretical background. The results and practical implications of both methods will be discussed in greater detail in subsequent chapters.

Conclusion

Neuropsychological intervention rests on the assumption that not only individual but also subtype differences exist when populations of dyslexic subjects are examined. These may usefully be harnessed to provide differentiated intervention so that observed deficiencies in text access, whether in accuracy or in fluency, can be addressed directly. The allocation to subtype and the intervention methods are the direct result of observation and analysis of the reading process in relation to the theoretical framework, which provides a strong link between the elements within the approach. Although it is recommended that a thorough analysis of the reading errors is undertaken prior to intervention techniques being initiated, the type of errors are usually so apparent that the reading behaviour can be deduced from skilful observation. The majority of teachers report that formal analysis merely confirms their perceptions of the reading behaviour and the reading deficits of pupils. This approach could make decisions on classification less important than decisions on the type of intervention to provide.

Chapter 4
Intervention method 1

Hemisphere-alluding stimulation

Hemisphere-alluding stimulation (HAS) can be delivered by adapting the text for the pupil so that the features of the text are manipulated, making the reading appeal more to one cerebral hemisphere than the opposing hemisphere. During the process of reading it has been demonstrated that many areas of the brain are activated, but by deliberately altering diverse elements of the text, it is possible to make the reading have a stronger appeal to one hemisphere. Figure 4.1 illustrates this.

SSSSSSSSSSSS
S
S
S
S
S
S

Figure 4.1 Differential response to a visual stimulus.

In this case when the focus is altered, different brain regions are engaged. Concentration on the 'T' created by the individual letters produces activity in the right hemisphere, while concentration on the 'S's causes activity in the left hemisphere. This has been demonstrated by positron emission tomography (PET) scans, which show how the different hemispheres react to diverse aspects of the same stimulus. It is almost impossible to isolate one hemisphere from another, even under strictly controlled situations, as the two hemispheres work in concert for most tasks, with many connections continually being made. It is, however, possible to engage one hemisphere more in a task by adapting the focus of the stimulus. During reading, the focus can be altered so that instead of appealing to both hemispheres, for example in the case of an L-type dyslexic subject, the text can be made more complex or unusual so that the reading refers to (or alludes to) the right hemisphere rather than the left. If the letters and words are made more complex, this evokes a need for the features of the letters themselves to be analysed. This concentration on the form and direction of the symbols requires more involvement of the right hemisphere (specialized for form and direction) in the reading process. Thus the right hemisphere becomes more actively engaged in the reading process. In the case of a P-type pupil, the text is modified so that a greater appeal is made to the left cerebral hemisphere and, as far as possible, elements that require greater involvement of the right cerebral hemisphere are deliberately omitted. Elements that might increase the involvement of the right hemisphere would include illustrations, use of colour and any complex letter fonts.

The appeal of HAS is that the materials can be delivered by a teacher to either an individual or a small group. A standard HAS session would include the pupil reading the specially adapted text to the teacher for 20-25 minutes and then performing exercises, again designed to stimulate the supposedly deficient hemisphere. Differentiated intervention is provided for the P- and the L-type dyslexic pupils in the following ways.

P (perceptual) subtypes

For this group the perceptual features of the text are in a conventional format. The text is printed in black ink on white paper, in a letter font familiar to the child to avoid any perceptual challenge. Illustrations are avoided in an attempt to focus on the linguistic as opposed to the pictorial message of the text. The text is adapted in the following ways:

1. Techniques are applied to the materials, which include deleting a number of words in the text as in a typical cloze procedure approach (Walker 1974). (Cloze procedure involves deleting words from text so that appropriate words can be inserted according to context. It is useful in encouraging active reader participation with text.) The pupil is then asked to supply the missing words. This is intended to raise the level of semantic skills of the pupils and to encourage reader–text interaction. It is also intended to reduce pupil dependence on the symbol (remembering that letter-by-letter reading can be a feature of this subtype) and to encourage the pupil to focus more on the message. The deleted words are immediately problematic for many P-type pupils, who require much encouragement to go beyond the deletion to access the meaning of the passage. They are often reluctant to guess, even when given guidance and supportive questioning.

2. Questions are asked about the meaning of certain words in the text during the actual reading. This again encourages pupil interaction with the meaning of the text.

3. Comprehension questions are posed when the reading is completed. These include factual questions on the subject matter and occasionally questions on the serial order of events in the story as this again is considered to allude more to left hemisphere processing. At the beginning of the session the pupils are informed that questions will follow the reading so they are prepared for the task.

An overriding principle is that inaccuracies should not become time-consuming as the assignments are designed to encourage fluent reading and to engage the pupil with the semantic aspect of the text.

Exercises.

For this group, exercises include activities aimed at improving phonological skills and these could include rhyming and 'odd one out' tasks (on the basis of phonic similarity). (Phonological skill is thought by most workers to be primarily a left hemisphere activity, but the role of phonology, particularly in respect of grapheme-phoneme correspondence, merits discussion with regard to the Balance Model, and this will be discussed in Chapter 8.) Some sentences contain words in the wrong order and the pupil is required to reassemble them in a way that makes sense. Other examples include the insertion of superfluous words in the text so that meaning is impeded. Pupil discussion on suitability is stressed to engage the pupil with the meaning aspect of the material (for examples of P-type materials see the second part of Appendix 2).

The overall aim of the reading for this subtype is to encourage fluent and speedy reading and to reduce reliance on the decoding of individual words. When pupils are reading the text they clearly find the deleted words difficult and need much encouragement to attempt to supply a word according to the context, as opposed to the actual symbols and letters.

L (linguistic) subtypes

This group is presented with text with the perceptual aspects highlighted in order to suppress the tendency for the pupil to read in a rushed or hurried fashion. The typography of the text can be adapted by, for example, mixing lower case and capitals of various dimensions in a word. Another modification uses a selection of fonts within a word. (It must be stated that such adaptation is time-consuming when performed on a standard word processor. It is possible to purchase a computer program in the Netherlands which adapts standard text to the required format. This program is called Scrambler and is available for both Apple Macintosh and IBM computers.) The revised texts are perceptually complex but still legible. The example in Figure 4.2 demonstrates both of the possible adaptations.

BeN wAs On HiS wAy To ScHoOl.

A liᴛᴛlE black dᴑg Was in the park

Figure 4.2 Adaptation of printed reading material.

Pupils of minimal reading ability should have less complex texts, but materials should be, as far as possible, age and interest-level appropriate. The pupil is prepared in advance for the unusual appearance of the text. If an error is made, the teacher alerts the pupil to the error and says 'Look closely and tell me again what it says'. The pupil should be given adequate time to attempt the unknown word but the teacher should supply the word if the pupil cannot read it. Sequences of cases, fonts and types are adapted according to the pupil's reading ability. Following the reading of the adapted text the pupil is given exercises which accentuate the perceptual features of the text. The exercises are again designed to encourage attention to the perceptual aspects of the letter symbols as opposed to the meaning of the text.

Exercises

- In a string of letters, both the lower case and the capital letters make a word. For example:

   PcLAYhGiROUldND   (PLAYGROUND / child)
   sLEtMOrNAaDEw   (LEMONADE / straw)

(vocabulary can be tailored to the appropriate reading level of the pupil).

- Word written in a corresponding shape to the object it represents, e.g. fish, smoke, etc.
- Figure/ground exercises finding concealed letters or words.
- Find the word. Arrange the words according to the size of the letters to find the word. For example:

   d a h (had).   g b i (big).

(Additional examples of L-type materials can be found in the first part of Appendix 2).

This intervention technique has proved popular and effective both with pupils and teachers and the detailed case studies included later in this chapter serve to highlight the different outcomes of the intervention according to pupil subtype.

In any discussion on intervention techniques, the priority is to consider the effects on individual pupils. It is also important to consider teachers' perceptions as to how user-friendly they find the materials, and to give teachers the opportunity to evaluate their perceptions of the value of materials to pupils. Often in reported studies only overall effects are given. These are useful in presenting a complete picture but do not allow the varied and individual pupil responses to be evaluated. In any intervention programmes it is useful to judge not only the effectiveness of the technique in terms of overall increases in standardized scores, but also how both sides of the teaching partnership perceive the materials. This section proposes to present individual results from some pupils in the study and to present both teacher and pupil comments on the intervention. This enables the method to be evaluated by not only the researcher but also by those responsible for providing support to individual pupils. The overall results of a range of studies using HAS will be presented in Chapter 6, but one from which the following case studies are drawn is presented briefly.

Robertson 1996

The sample for this study was selected from pupils within three local education authorities (LEAs) and all were statemented under the Code of Practice for the identification and assessment of pupils with special educational needs (DES, now DfEE, 1994). All were pupils who attended mainstream primary and secondary schools and support was provided by specialist teachers. Individual provision took place by withdrawing the pupils from mainstream lessons for periods of time ranging from 40 minutes to one hour.

The study took place over a period of 12 weeks on a sample of 37 pupils aged between 7 and 13 years. The study involved the author (as one of the providers of the teaching) and 15 teachers who had volunteered to take part. Prior to intervention the pupils were tested using the Neale Analysis of Reading Ability (NARA) (Neale 1989).

It was expected that a selection of mini-case studies might reveal the impact of the approach for certain pupils (and their teachers) and both teacher and pupil comments were included. On an individual case study level, the improvement for certain pupils was considerable. These examples have been selected to demonstrate the impact on pupils for whom the HAS approach was successful, although it can be seen that individual results across measures of accuracy, comprehension, rate of reading and the pattern of errors do show individual variation.

Case study 1: Adam

Adam was a boy of 13 years and 6 months. He had been assessed at the age of 10 years as having specific learning difficulties – the preferred term for dyslexia within the LEA where he attended school. When support began he had very little independent reading ability, limited sight vocabulary, and minimal independent spelling ability. Teaching was delivered by multisensory methods and followed the

Hickey Multisensory Language Course (Augur and Briggs 1994). Progress was steady but slow and support was continued when he transferred to secondary school at the age of 11 years. His approach to text was hurried and he was often criticized within the school setting for carelessness. This was how it appeared, but in fact this was not the case. In reality he exerted maximum effort into any reading task and was highly motivated to achieve, despite his initial experience of failure. His reading behaviour was fast and showed evidence of misreading even those words that were known to be within his sight vocabulary. Usually the words substituted would bear a superficial visual similarity to the initial stimulus. Explicit sound–symbol conversion of unknown words was attempted only for those initial letter sounds and blends that had been taught within the framework of the multisensory programme. Explicit decoding was clearly not a preferred style and would usually take place only when encouraged by his teacher. From a neuropsychological perspective his reading showed some elements of the L-type approach to text. This was subsequently confirmed by assessment and the results can be found in Table 4.1.

Table 4.1 Pre-intervention testing (Neale Analysis of Reading Ability, NARA) on pupil Adam, 13 years 6 months

Chronological age	13.06 years	
Reading age (accuracy)	6.02 years	(raw score 22)
Reading age (comprehension)	7.02 years	(raw score 12)
Reading age (rate)	8.05 years	(raw score 63)
Substantive errors	41	
Fragmentation errors	5	

The reading accuracy score shows an overall decrement of almost seven years in comparison to his chronological age. Reading comprehension is slightly higher, but rate of reading is higher still. This revealed a classically L-type profile. The reading accuracy score was clearly affected by many inaccurate responses to the text. Most of the errors were of the substantive type and revealed an inaccurate response to the perceptual or visual aspects of the text. These included the reversal of 'was' for 'saw' and two instances that demonstrate a superficial visual similarity ('talking' for 'taking' and 'panted' for 'pointing'). (A sample of the results for this pupil can be seen in the example of error analysis for pupil A, in Chapter 3.)

Intervention was provided to stimulate the right (mainly perceptual) hemisphere and took place over 13 weeks at one session per week of approximately 35 minutes' duration. Materials were as far as possible age and interest-level appropriate. Post-testing was carried out five months later and the results can be found in Table 4.2.

The pupil reported that he felt the material had helped him with his reading but he could not be more specific as to the nature of the improvement. His teacher

Table 4.2 Post-intervention testing (Neale Analysis of Reading Ability, NARA) on pupil Adam, 13 years 11 months

Reading age (accuracy)	6.07 years	(raw score 27)
Reading age (comprehension)	7.02 years	(raw score 12)
Rate of reading could not be assessed on this occasion.		
Substantive errors	26	
Fragmentation errors	5	

also confirmed that there appeared to be a more careful response to text, though this was not so evident in the assessment results. These results were disappointing in terms of overall increase but may best be evaluated by considering the initial deficit in reading accuracy. It is also noteworthy that while Adam was receiving the intervention, reading accuracy age increased by five months, which was more than the length of time of intervention (five months against 13 weeks of intervention). There is also a reduction in the number of substantive errors in this assessment (26 as opposed to 41).

Intervention then ceased by the HAS method but testing on the NARA took place six months later. The follow-up testing was considered important to gauge the durability of any improvement as it was considered that if the intervention was effective, results should demonstrate lasting effects.

Follow-up testing took place immediately following the long summer holiday when Adam was 14 years and 2 months. Many teachers acknowledge retention of learning following a school holiday as being problematic, as it may occasion a short-term regression of reading ability, possibly due to less exposure to print during holiday time. The results were surprising (see Table 4.3).

These results showed that not only had the initial increase in reading accuracy been maintained, but had actually increased (by five months) in the period of three months when there had been no direct intervention, and possibly very little reading generally. Raw scores for reading accuracy were now 32 (against the original 22 at pre-testing and 27 at post-testing). Another interesting result is that the pattern of errors had changed, with an almost negligible reduction of substantive errors (25 as opposed to 26) but an increase in fragmentation errors (15 against 5 on both the pre-

Table 4.3 Follow-up testing (Neale Analysis of Reading Ability, NARA) on pupil Adam, 14 years and 2 months

Reading age (accuracy)	7.00 years	(raw score 32)
Reading age (comprehension)	8.02 years	(raw score 16)
Reading age (rate)	6.08 years	(raw score 44)
Substantive errors	25	
Fragmentation errors	15	

intervention and post-intervention testing). In terms of the theoretical framework this may signal a different response to text and the beginnings of perceptual care towards printed material. Reading had also slowed down (demonstrated by a change in the rate of reading age of more than one and a half years). This slower reading was a desirable outcome for this pupil as it allowed time for perceptual analysis of the text to take place. These apparent changes were found not only when reading special HAS materials but were reported by his teacher as being evident in many reading contexts. This information was particularly welcome, as support teachers often report problems of transfer of learning from a support to a classroom context.

Case study 2: James

James was 12 years old and attended a mainstream secondary school. For two years he had been in receipt of individual withdrawal support from a teacher with a qualification in supporting dyslexic pupils. When support began he had some independent reading ability, limited sight vocabulary and minimal independent spelling ability. Teaching was delivered by multisensory methods and followed the Hickey Multisensory Language Course (Augur and Briggs 1994). Progress was steady but slow, and support had continued when he transferred to secondary school at the age of 11 years. When the HAS intervention began he had a reading accuracy age (NARA) of 7 years and 8 months and a reading comprehension age of 9 years and 8 months (see Table 4.4). This is not surprising, as his approach to text was hurried and, superficially, his reading appeared careless, with many errors of function words. Analysis of the results of the Boder Test of Reading and Spelling patterns (Boder and Jarrico 1982) yielded a dysphonetic pattern and showed difficulty accessing words by the indirect route. Although the utility of this test has been criticized in terms of classification outcomes, it can provide a useful perspective on the differential abilities in reading and spelling both known and unknown words. From a neuropsychological perspective, superficially his reading showed some elements of the L-type approach to text, in which a hurried response was made to unknown words, usually on the basis of surface similarities. Examples taken from the single-word reading of the Boder Test show this, e.g. 'charity' for 'character', 'dictionary' for 'dictation' and 'horrible' for 'honourable'.

Table 4.4 Pre-intervention testing (Neale Analysis of Reading Ability, NARA) on pupil James, 12 years 1 month

Chronological age	12.01 years	
Reading age (accuracy)	7.08 years	(raw score 39)
Reading age (comprehension)	9.08 years	(raw score 22)
Reading age (rate)	8.09 years.	(raw score 67)
Substantive errors	18	
Fragmentation errors	18	

Table 4.4 shows first an overall decrement of more than four years in reading accuracy when compared to his chronological age. The score for reading comprehension is substantially higher and shows that the pupil had good access to the meaning of the passage despite any reading errors. Rate of reading is also higher than reading accuracy, but lower than reading comprehension. This demonstrates the fast but inaccurate reading behaviour of this pupil.

Error analysis according to the Bakker classification system showed a mixed profile, as there were equivalent substantive and fragmentation errors (in both cases 18). The decrement of more than four years in his reading accuracy age against his chronological age had surprisingly little apparent impact on his self-esteem. When the errors were analysed, most of the fragmentation errors were self-corrections and showed careful attention to the meaning of the text. Most of the inaccurate responses to the perceptual or visual aspects of the text were still in keeping with the central meaning of the text.

As the pupil had an error profile that showed substantive and fragmentation errors in equal proportions, it would have been theoretically possible to use materials to stimulate either cerebral hemisphere. In the event, the research design of the study necessitated using HAS materials for the left hemisphere (P-type materials). This was due to the initial classification of the pupil sample into subtypes revealing few P-types but several pupils who made equivalent numbers of substantive and fragmentation errors. The research design was therefore amended to investigate whether these pupils (designated M-types) showed different responses to the materials. (The reasons for this are expanded Chapter 6.) It was expected that this would capitalize on the existing good strategies for semantic and syntactic interaction with the text, but it was thought that it might reveal differential effects from the L-type materials involving more right hemisphere tasks.

James subsequently received stimulation of the left hemisphere via the adapted text. He was a willing student, co-operative with all tasks and was well motivated in his support lessons. He responded well to the intervention materials and completed the full 13 sessions using the materials. His teacher reported that, by the end of the 13 weeks, he was getting a little bored with the materials, but was still co-operative. Testing immediately following the intervention revealed changes, which in view of his previous long-term support (more than two years) with multisensory methods may be attributed to the HAS intervention (see Table 4.5).

Table 4.5 Post-intervention testing (Neale Analysis of Reading Ability, NARA) on pupil James, 12 years 5 months

Chronological age	12.05 years	
Reading age (accuracy)	9.11 years	(raw score 62)
Reading age (comprehension)	12.03 years	(raw score 31)
Rate of reading could not be assessed on this occasion		
Substantive errors	17	
Fragmentation errors	8	

Post-testing for this pupil showed a reading accuracy score of 9.11 years (an increase of 2 years and 3 months) and a comprehension score of 12 years and 3 months (an increase of 2 years and 7 months). These results were surprising as the P-type materials are thought to impact more on reading fluency than on reading accuracy, yet the gains for this pupil had been substantial. In real terms, both James and his support teacher had noted a great improvement in his general reading ability and this was not only noticeable with the specifically adapted text, but had clearly transferred to all reading tasks. The pupil reported that he felt the material had helped him with his reading but he did not know how. It is also noteworthy that while James was receiving the intervention, his reading accuracy age had increased by 2 years and 3 months against 13 weeks of intervention. Comprehension in the same period had increased by 2 years and 7 months. It is unfortunate that changes in rate of reading could not be computed on this occasion.

When the pattern of errors was analysed according to the Bakker criteria, they revealed changes that supported the theoretical position. The number of fragmentation errors had decreased, which could show improved reading fluency. Despite the improvement in reading accuracy, the number of substantive errors had not decreased but the teacher commented on the reduction in the number of miscues apparent in his general text reading.

Intervention then ceased by the HAS method but testing on the NARA took place six months later, again following the long summer holiday. The results can be found in Table 4.6. These results showed that not only had the initial increase in reading accuracy been maintained, but had actually increased in the absence of any direct intervention. Another interesting result is that the pattern of errors had changed with an overall reduction in the number of fragmentation errors. In terms of the theoretical framework this may signal an improvement of fluency in response to text. Reading had also slowed down, which again was a surprising outcome for this pupil, as this is not usually a consequence of HAS stimulation of the left cerebral hemisphere.

Results on this occasion yielded a reading accuracy score of 10 years and 4 months (an increase of 5 months albeit in a period without specific intervention)

Table 4.6 Follow-up testing (Neale Analysis of Reading Ability, NARA) on pupil James, 12 years 8 months

Chronological age	12.08 years	
Reading age (accuracy)	10.04 years	(raw score 66)
Reading age (comprehension)	13+ years (ceiling level of instrument)	(raw score 34)
Reading age (rate)	7.09 years	(raw score 56)
Substantive errors	19	
Fragmentation errors	8	

and a comprehension age of 13+ years (the pupil had reached the ceiling level of the measurement instrument). There had thus been an overall increase of 2 years 6 months in accuracy and more than 3 years 4 months in comprehension, both being viewed very positively by pupil and teacher alike.

These two case studies serve to highlight apparent differences as a result of differential intervention. Adam increased in reading accuracy and showed a different error profile, with a reduction in the number of substantive errors. This would be justified according to the theory of the intervention, which had targeted the right cerebral hemisphere. In marked contrast James had gained not only in reading accuracy and reading comprehension but showed a significant reduction in the number of fragmentation errors revealed by the reading. These two brief case studies describe differentiated intervention via the medium of adapted text. The results of larger-scale studies are reported in Chapter 6. They highlight the individual variation that may occur following neuropsychological intervention. Other cases will be presented briefly to allow other differential outcomes to be revealed. Although the changes are not consistently in the expected areas, they serve to demonstrate the gains that can be made for certain pupils. The differential effects on the various dimensions of the reading process can be highlighted by reference to another pupil, Lee.

Case study 3: Lee

Lee attended a mainstream secondary school and was aged 11 years and 6 months when first tested. Again, he had been receiving specialist support for approximately two years. Table 4.7 shows the pre-test results for this pupil.

On the NARA he scored a reading accuracy age of 7 years 2 months and a comprehension age of 7 years and 11 months. Once again, there is a large discrepancy between chronological age and reading accuracy age. The rate of reading reveals the slow reading style of this pupil. This, along with the number of fragmentation errors, suggested he was a P-type pupil. In this case the number of substantive errors was higher than would be expected. Analysis of the reading errors according to the Bakker criteria again yielded a mixed pattern, as Lee made

Table 4.7 Pre-intervention testing (Neale Analysis of Reading Ability, NARA) on pupil Lee, 11 years 6 months

Chronological age	11.06 years	
Reading age (accuracy)	7.02 years	(raw score 33)
Reading age (comprehension)	7.11 years	(raw score 17)
Reading age (rate)	5.07 years	(raw score 30)
Substantive errors	30	
Fragmentation errors	27	

30 substantive errors and 27 fragmentation errors. In view of the equivalence in the type of reading errors it was decided to stimulate the left hemisphere to attempt to increase the fluency of the response to text. Lee subsequently completed all 13 intervention sessions using the HAS materials. His teacher reported that he had struggled with the reading materials and tended to over-compensate for the difficulty with the materials. He experienced particular problems with the cloze procedure text and could not react with any confidence. Consequently, his reading during intervention became even slower and more stilted. He was more positive and confident about the exercises following the reading and was reported as enjoying both the story sequencing and rhyming activities, experiencing considerable success with them. After the intervention period of 13 weeks, testing was carried out and the results are given in Table 4.8.

Testing here revealed a reading accuracy score of 7 years 11 months (an increase of 9 months) and a reading comprehension score of 8 years 2 months (an almost negligible increase of 3 months). The comprehension results clearly surprised his teacher, who had noted improved reading in different contexts. His teacher had anticipated that access to the meaning of the text would also have improved. Detailed error analysis again revealed an almost equal number of errors of each type; in fact the number of errors had increased from the first occasion of testing.

HAS intervention then ceased and follow-up testing was carried out immediately following the summer holiday (again an interval of 6 months). The results showed the same pattern of increases after direct intervention had ceased as had been noted with other subjects (see Table 4.9).

Table 4.8 Post-intervention testing (Neale Analysis of Reading Ability, NARA) on pupil Lee, 11 years 11 months

Chronological age	11.09 years	
Reading age (accuracy)	7.11 years	(raw score 42)
Reading age (comprehension)	8.02 years	(raw score 16)
Reading age (rate)	7.06 years	(raw score 52)
Substantive errors	45	
Fragmentation errors	43	

Table 4.9 Follow-up testing (Neale Analysis of Reading Ability, NARA) on pupil Lee, 12 years 5 months

Chronological age	12.05 years	
Reading age (accuracy)	8.05 years	(raw score 47)
Reading age (comprehension)	9.11 years	(raw score 23)
Reading age (rate)	5.07 years	(raw score 28)
Substantive errors	26	
Fragmentation errors	20	

On this occasion, Lee gained a reading accuracy score of 8 years 5 months (an increase of 6 months). As with the other cases this was again immediately following a period without specific intervention and including the summer vacation. A comprehension age of 9 years 11 months was achieved (an increase of 1 year 9 months on the last comprehension result). Analysis of reading errors showed a reduction of both substantive and fragmentation errors, which could herald some change of approach to text but which was not only in the expected direction. (P-type materials do not usually impact on the number of substantive errors.)

In both of the last cases (pupils James and Lee) gains in reading accuracy were evident, despite the intervention materials being designed to increase fluency rather than accuracy of reading. There are therefore some pupil and treatment interaction effects, which cannot always be predicted from the theory but which are significant for the pupils. Any improvements also need to be evaluated alongside the original discrepancy against chronological age. The extent of the improvements can be deemed significant for the dyslexic pupil, for whom a month-by-month increase in reading accuracy and reading comprehension may be an unrealistic expectation. Both these pupils had also been in receipt of multisensory teaching for at least two years, so it is possible to infer that the neuropsychological intervention may have been a significant factor in the increases. However, it must be acknowledged that this is speculation.

It is interesting to compare these results with those of pupils who received intervention via the L-type materials, which are designed to impact more on reading accuracy, and the results of two pupils will be presented briefly to enable comparisons to be made.

Case study 4: Lewis

Lewis attended a mainstream secondary school and was 12 years and 6 months old when the HAS intervention began. He had also been in receipt of long-term multisensory teaching from a specialist support teacher. The results can be seen in the Table 4.10.

Table 4.10 Pre-intervention testing (Neale Analysis of Reading Ability, NARA) on pupil Lewis, 12 years 6 months

Chronological age	12.06 years	
Reading age (accuracy)	8.07 years	(raw score 49)
Reading age (comprehension)	12.03 years	(raw score 31)
Reading age (rate)	not assessed	
Substantive errors	71	
Fragmentation errors	31	

On initial testing, the results for this pupil yielded a reading accuracy age of 8 years and 7 months and a comprehension age of 12 years and 3 months. This is a large discrepancy and may indicate that, for this pupil, there were more strategies available for text comprehension than the low reading accuracy score would indicate. Analysis of reading errors revealed a total of 71 substantive errors, but only 31 fragmentation errors. This reveals a marked L-type profile so the theoretically appropriate (that is the right) hemisphere was selected for stimulation. The teacher reported that the pupil read the adapted text with little difficulty but that it did slow down his rate of reading considerably. The teacher observed that over the 10 weeks of intervention the pupil increased both in fluency and skill with the supplementary exercises. He found the reading challenging but was well motivated and persevered with all tasks. (This pupil received only 10 of the 13 possible sessions due to school absence.) The results after only 10 sessions of the HAS materials were surprising and supported the perceptions of both the teacher and the pupil that there had been an improvement in his reading skill (see Table 4.11).

The subsequent testing had yielded a reading accuracy age of 10 years and 1 month (an increase of 1 year and 6 months) and a reading comprehension age of 13+ years (the pupil had reached the ceiling level of the instrument). It was clear that the number of substantive errors in particular had decreased and again it was considered that this could demonstrate an improved attention to the perceptual details of the text. The number of fragmentation errors had remained almost constant. The results of the final testing for this pupil (Table 4.12) confirmed the gains that had been made in his reading and it could be presumed that this had been occasioned by the introduction of the HAS intervention technique.

Table 4.11 Post-intervention testing (Neale Analysis of Reading Ability, NARA) on pupil Lewis, 12 years 9 months

Chronological age	12.09 years	
Reading age (accuracy)	10.01 years	(raw score 63)
Reading age (comprehension)	13+ years	(raw score 35)
Reading age (rate)	not assessed	
Substantive errors	39	
Fragmentation errors	34	

Table 4.12 Follow-up testing (Neale Analysis of Reading Ability, NARA) on pupil Lewis, 13 years 1 month

Chronological age	13.01 years	
Reading age (accuracy)	10.06 years	(raw score 67)
Reading age (comprehension)	13+ years	(raw score 35)
Reading age (rate)	not assessed	
Substantive errors	20	
Fragmentation errors	11	

Final testing after 16 weeks without intervention yielded a reading accuracy score of 10 years and 6 months (an increase of five months, which is one month above the time period between testing) with reading comprehension again at the ceiling level of the instrument. For this pupil there was still a discrepancy of reading accuracy against both chronological age and reading comprehension but this had decreased considerably. An interesting feature of the results for this pupil is revealed when the reading errors are analysed, as both types of reading errors decreased steadily between the occasions of testing. From the initial profile of 71 substantive and 31 fragmentation errors, the results on the second occasion of testing were 39 and 34 errors of each type and by the final occasion of testing this had decreased further to 20 substantive errors and 11 fragmentation errors. The reduction in substantive errors was not unexpected and is reflected in the improved reading accuracy score. It could signal that, for this pupil, his approach to text had changed as a result of the intervention, but the decrease in fragmentation errors is not easily explained by reference to the theory. A possibility is that pupil confidence in the reading task had increased as a result of the success he was experiencing, and this made his reading more fluent.

Case study 5: Alan

This is again a pupil who, on the basis of the Bakker error analysis, received the theoretically appropriate intervention (via the L-type materials). Alan was a pupil of 13 years and 8 months, who attended a mainstream secondary school and who was also in receipt of individual withdrawal support. Pre-testing results for Alan are shown in Table 4.13.

This pupil, on initial testing, yielded a reading accuracy age of 7 years and 2 months and a reading comprehension age of 7 years and 8 months. Initial error analysis yielded 12 substantive errors and 9 fragmentation errors. Alan again revealed a mixed profile making it theoretically valid to stimulate either the right or the left cerebral hemisphere. Subsequent discussions with his support teacher confirmed that it would be more appropriate to stimulate the right hemisphere, as his reading was noticeably perceptually careless. This decision was also considered

Table 4.13 Pre-intervention testing (Neale Analysis of Reading Ability, NARA) on pupil Alan, 13 years 8 months

Chronological age	13.08 years	
Reading age (accuracy)	7.02 years	(raw score 33)
Reading age (comprehension)	7.08 years	(raw score 14)
Reading age (rate)	6.02 years	(raw score 38)
Substantive errors	12	
Fragmentation errors	9	

appropriate on consideration of a reading accuracy age decrement of 6 years and 6 months against chronological age. This suggested that the developmental model of aiming to increase perceptual care towards the written text would be advisable. The pupil responded positively to both the adapted text and the exercises and testing after 13 intervention sessions showed positive results (see Table 4.14).

Reading accuracy had increased to 8 years and 4 months (an increase of 1 year and 2 months) and reading comprehension had increased to 9 years and 8 months (an increase of 2 years). This was a result expected by his support teacher, who had commented on the gains she felt had been made in his general reading ability. Error analysis was difficult to interpret as Alan had reached the next level of the graded reading passages of the NARA so understandably had made more errors than in his pre-test results. It can also be seen that the proportion of errors of each type has changed and now fragmentation errors are more frequent. This could also indicate that the pupil approach to text had changed as reading rate has also decreased. Again intervention by HAS ceased and follow-up testing was carried out after 6 months (see Table 4.15).

By follow-up testing the gains were not only maintained but extended, as accuracy was now 8 years and 9 months (an increase of 5 months) and comprehension 10 years and 2 months (an increase of 6 months). Error analysis was problematic, as on the last occasion of testing, the pupil had reached level 4 of the graded reading passages, whereas on initial testing he had reached only level 2. If the first two passages only are compared, the substantive errors had decreased

Table 4.14 Post-intervention testing (Neale Analysis of Reading Ability, NARA) on pupil Alan, 13 years 11 months

Chronological age	13.11 years	
Reading age (accuracy)	8.04 years	(raw score 46)
Reading age (comprehension)	9.08 years	(raw score 22)
Reading age (rate)	5.00 years	
Substantive errors	39	
Fragmentation errors	99	

Table 4.15 Follow-up testing (Neale Analysis of Reading Ability, NARA) on pupil Alan, 14 years 5 months

Chronological age	14.05 years	
Reading age (accuracy)	8.09 years	(raw score 50)
Reading age (comprehension)	10.02 years	(raw score 24)
Reading age (rate)	7.04 years	(raw score 46)
Substantive errors	31	
Fragmentation errors	45	

from 12 to 2 and fragmentation errors from 9 to 4. Analysis for the more difficult passages (passages 3 and 4) showed 30 substantive and 45 fragmentation errors. This is interesting, as now the pupil would have been classified altogether differently and would have been given stimulation of the left hemisphere to increase fluency. This has an important message regarding the interaction between text level and reader, but may also signal a change of approach to reading and an increase in perceptual care towards the alphabetic symbols and increased facility in manipulating them.

Such results demonstrate the utility of the approach for certain pupils, but also demonstrate the important treatment × pupil interactions that may emerge. One factor of interest is the differences in results for individuals. This was highlighted in a report of two case studies (Kappers and Bos 1990). The subjects were both male, had been classified as P-type dyslexics and had discrepancies in reading age against chronological age of 3.5 years (pupil C) and 6.5 years (pupil M). Both boys were noted as lacking motivation to reading tasks (which is hardly surprising) and had received specialist intervention in a special school for four years (pupil C) and six years (pupil M). Both had been assessed as being low average to average ability on the Wechsler Intelligence Scale for Children-Revised (WISC-R; Wechsler 1976). In this study, both boys received two periods of HAS treatment. The first comprised nine sessions of HAS intervention (three sessions per week) using materials to stimulate the right hemisphere. The second phase of intervention was again nine sessions, but this time included stimulation of the left hemisphere via the auditory channel. This was accomplished by the boys hearing the voice of the therapist and their own voice in the right ear. The left ear simultaneously received soft instrumental music. The adaptation to include the auditory channel was achieved by specially adapted headphones and an amplifier. The aim of this treatment was therefore to improve reading performance through activation of the left cerebral hemisphere. Reading was assessed at various points in the intervention programme and the results for both boys were in the predicted direction. Both had increases in their rate of reading and decreases in the number of time-consuming errors in their reading. It was interesting that both these effects were stable one month and one year after the intervention ceased for only one boy (case C). In the case of pupil M, the effects disappeared completely at the end of the treatment. Kappers concluded that identical treatments, which appear to be indicated for children with similar reading problems, need not lead to similar results. In the case of left hemisphere HAS, there can be positive results or negligible results. Thus, after intervention of nine weeks (for one pupil) there appeared to be a persistent shift in reading style, which suggested increased involvement of the left hemisphere. Reading speed had increased and the number of time-consuming errors had decreased. Kappers speculates that the HAS intervention is possibly different from remedial approaches, in that it is a correctional approach which tries to correct the underlying mode of information processing. (No clear conclusions were drawn on the supplementary effects of the stimulation via the right ear.)

Conclusion

In conclusion, the presentation of results for individual pupils may demonstrate that HAS intervention can be helpful in increasing the reading skill of certain pupils with entrenched reading difficulties. Results suggest that HAS can allow certain aptitude × instruction interactions of utility to be identified, but these may not always be in the predicted areas. It may prove an alternative treatment medium, through which intervention may be directed at assessed strengths and weaknesses in the reading process. It may allow pupils to benefit by differentiated intervention being provided through more individually designed programmes, so that in the case of pupils with the M-type profile they can first receive stimulation of the right cerebral hemisphere to consolidate the perceptual importance of the symbols. This could then be followed by stimulation of the left cerebral hemisphere to facilitate semantic access to the text. Such procedures may also illuminate possible extensions of the work so that initial stimulation of one hemisphere may be followed by a second period of intervention to stimulate the opposing hemisphere. This would address the need for the development of both accuracy and fluency in successful reading. This work is currently being pursued in the specialist reading clinics in the Netherlands.

One factor of importance could be the revealed increases after direct intervention has ceased. Many teachers of pupils with dyslexia note that retention of learned material may be problematic following a holiday of even a week's duration. This finding was not unique to these studies, as other studies in neuropsychological intervention have reported similar findings. These will be discussed more fully in Chapter 6.

Chapter 5
Intervention method 2

Hemisphere-specific stimulation

Hemisphere-specific stimulation (HSS) can be delivered either by computer, using the visual half-fields (HSS visual), or by a tactile method (HSS tactile).

Computer-delivered HSS

HSS visual is delivered via the visual half-fields and involves the use of a fixation point. Words are flashed in the left or right of the periphery depending on which hemisphere is being targeted. The fixation point is an important element in ensuring access to the visual half-fields. In HSS visual there is a demonstration of the crossover relationship between field and hemisphere, as the words flashed in the right visual field activate the left cerebral hemisphere. Conversely, words flashed in the left visual field activate the right cerebral hemisphere. Intervention can therefore be tailored to maximize the involvement of one hemisphere over the other. In both cases, presentation times are less than 300 milliseconds to prevent overt decoding.

A commercial program (Hemstim) has been devised to deliver HSS training via the visual half-field (Bakker and Vonk 1998). Intervention can be differentiated, as the program allows the duration of the flashed stimulus to become increasingly shorter, depending on the performance of the subject. The words targeted for decoding are entered by the program user and can thus be tailored for use with different languages. Vocabulary can also be tailored according to the independent reading level of the pupil and can be made age and interest-level appropriate. Word properties are also adjusted differentially. Concrete or imageable words are used for the L-types, which encourages greater involvement of the right hemisphere. In contrast, abstract words are used for P-types, which has been found to encourage greater involvement of the left cerebral hemisphere. This was found problematic, as words of low readability were often found by the writer to be concrete, whereas abstract words were found to demand better reading ability. Following the trend of the theory, words are flashed to the left visual half-field of L-type pupils and the right visual half-field of the P-type pupils (see Figure 5.1).

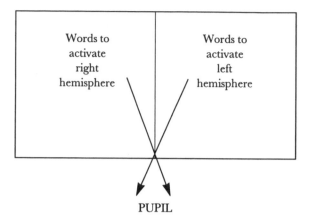

Figure 5.1 Demonstrating HSS visual.

To gain access to the HSS program, words are flashed on to the computer screen while the pupil is fixated on the centre of the screen. Fixation is achieved by the pupil focusing attention on a small box in the centre of the screen and attempting to direct a moving cross into it. Operating the computer mouse controls the moving cross and when the pupil succeeds in placing the cross in the box both central images disappear and a word flashes into the appropriate visual half-field. The mouse speed can also be adjusted, although it is deliberately set on an erratic course to ensure fixation time.

In one study (Johnson and Robertson 1999), pupils first decoded individual words and then carried out various activities, such as making decisions on whether pairs of words were the same or different, or spelling aloud the words they had seen. In general, pupils were very positive about the intervention and enjoyed working on the computer. Experimental results are presented in a Chapter 5.

An additional benefit of the Hemstim program is that pupil records are stored in the computer and can be accessed by a teacher to reveal any progress. This can inform teaching decisions as to whether fixation times or mouse speed are in need of adjustment in the event of pupil performance improving. It also allows a teacher to alter the level of the words in the light of improved performance.

HSS tactile

In this method, reading material is presented via the touch (tactile) receptors of the hands. The aim is to present all materials by touch and not by sight. To this end a tactile training box is used and this can be seen in Figure 5.2.

This was constructed according to the specifications of Bakker (1990). It had a width of approximately 60 centimetres, a depth of approximately 55 centimetres and a largest and smallest height of 30 and 15 centimetres respectively. An opening

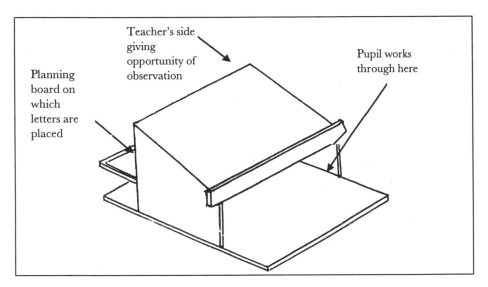

Figure 5.2 Tactile training box.

approximately 10 centimetres high, over the total width of the tactile training box, appears on the pupil's side; on the teacher's side the opening is approximately 25 centimetres high. On the pupil's side of the box strips of wood have been placed under the floor and at the sides. These strips are slightly thicker than the total thickness of the planning board, including the letters (or other materials) that are fastened to it. The thick strip of wood is omitted on the teacher's side of the floor so there is an open space between the floor of the box and the surface on which it has been placed, e.g. table, desk, etc.; the planning board can be placed in this open space. The words and sentences can therefore be placed on the planning board and pushed under the floor of the box so that only the first row of material is exposed. The words and sentences also need to be fixed in position so that the child does not move the sequence while touching the letters. Once the pupil has worked through the first row of material, the board can be pulled out to reveal subsequent rows of material. The planning boards used were 30 centimetres wide and 40 centimetres deep. The pupil should be prevented from seeing the last row, so it is necessary to indent the floor of the box on the teacher's side. The pupil should be able to sit comfortably behind the tactile training box. The height of the chair should be such that the elbow of the arm the child puts into the box can rest comfortably on the floor of the box.

The construction of the box is such that the teacher has an unimpeded view of the pupil's movements throughout. This allows detailed observation and analysis of the pupil's reading behaviour, which can be diagnostically significant. When observing the pupils, subtype differences can be identified immediately. The P-type pupil classically palpates the letter on numerous occasions before attempting to name the letter aloud. In contrast, the L-type pupil makes a very hurried response on the basis of minimal information. An example of this was observed with many pupils involved in the experimental work who, on feeling a downstroke of a letter would name the letter as 't', for example. It was then pointed out that on the information available the letter could have been any of the letters containing a downstroke, such as 't', 'f', 'l', 'k', 'h', 'b' or even 'd'. A similarly fast and inappropriate response was frequently observed on making decisions as to whether words were the same or different. Often the pupil would make a decision after only one word had been palpated! Another noticeable feature of the L-type pupils was an understandable reluctance to use the left hand (all were right-handed) and all were sure the task would be much easier if they could use the preferred hand. In one case the pupil was allowed to do this briefly at the end of a teaching session and was duly surprised that using his preferred hand yielded no advantage.

Treatment procedure

Pupils are given a range of tasks, the most important of these always being the palpation of letters, words and sentences with the left hand in the case of the L-type dyslexic pupil and the right hand in the case of the P-type dyslexic pupil. This can be done in a variety of ways, but the method preferred by Bakker is with the index and/or middle finger. (The author adhered to this procedure.)

Main tasks

In all cases an over-riding consideration was readability and all material presented to the hands was at the independent reading level for the pupils. All pupils were given an introductory session, in which they had the opportunity to familiarize themselves with the technique.

1. Letters/words and sentences are identified first by touch and then named aloud. The pupil reads out words and sentences after the entire word/sentence has been palpated. This is to discourage the L-type pupil from guessing after only part of the item has been palpated. As far as possible for the L-type pupil, words are concrete and imageable, as this involves the right hemisphere more directly. Conversely, the P-type pupil is presented with abstract words. This is problematic: abstract words tend to have a higher readability age than concrete words.
2. A letter or figure plate is placed on the slanted (desk) side of the tactile training box. A palpated letter or word is then compared with, for example, four different words or figures on the plate. The pupil can then be questioned as to which word is the same as the word he or she has just felt. To add variety, words, letters, etc., can be written on the pupil's fingers or palms of the hand or the pupil can be asked to write the palpated stimulus in the air or on a piece of paper (using the same hand as is used for palpation of the letters).

As with the HAS treatment, the level of difficulty of the task should be matched with the pupil's ability. Regardless of ability, however, sessions should always commence with the presentation of individual capital letters, followed by individual lower case letters and then simple and more complex groups of letters forming words. This was adhered to for both L- and P-types.

Differential treatments

P-types (using right hand to stimulate left cerebral hemisphere)

1. Words/sentences are presented with letters or words omitted and it is the pupil's task to fill in the gaps. The pupil is encouraged to go beyond the perceived 'gap' in the word to the next letter and to attempt to fill in the missing components on the basis of meaning or context. When pupils were carrying out this task it was clear they found it difficult not to focus solely on the micro aspects of the symbol but to go beyond this to the macro aspect of the meaning.
2. Questions are posed regarding serial (temporal) positions of letters in a word or of words in a sentence. This was included because temporal order is thought to involve the left hemisphere more directly.
3. The pupil palpates a word, e.g. 'need', and is asked which of the following words (called out by the teacher) is equivalent to the palpated word, e.g. 'nod', 'feed' or 'need'.
4. The pupil palpates a word and is asked to supply a rhyming word. Again, this is intended to increase the involvement of the left hemisphere.
5. The pupil palpates a word and is asked to find a written representation of the word from a series of words presented by the teacher.
6. For P-types, abstract words should be used as much as possible to appeal to the left hemisphere. Words should also be perceptually simple so simple letter-forms and fonts are used.

There now follows a description of a session delivered to a P-type pupil, who is in the early stages of literacy development. In this case the equipment was the tactile training box and the letters were presented on a board such as those found giving conference details, etc. This has the advantage of allowing the letters to be fixed in place so they are not inadvertently moved by the pupil while he or she is palpating the letters.

Example of a P-type lesson (early stages)

Naming words

In this first activity the pupil merely reads the letters aloud after feeling all the letters.

1. have
2. said
3. much
4. for
5. with
6. came
7. back
8. like
9. made
10. then

Sentences

After palpating the individual words, the pupil is informed that the words are now in full sentences. The teacher should monitor the pupil to make sure that he or she is palpating the words individually and is aware of the spaces between the words. This is to avoid the pupil trying to read two words as one. After the reading of each sentence, the pupil is asked questions on the serial order of the words in the sentence, for example 'What was the second word/third word, etc.?' (serial order being a left hemisphere activity).

1. That is my house.
2. The dog is not well.
3. He ran in the park.
4. I will get on the bus.
5. Mum will look sad.

Deletions

The activity for the pupil again changes and this time he or she is presented with sentences with certain letters deleted. The teacher again needs to monitor that the pupil is aware of the word boundaries and, in the case of missing letters in the middle of words, is encouraged to go beyond the gap and to make an informed decision as to what the missing letter and, subsequently, the word is. At this point in the session the pupil response is judged on accuracy for semantic acceptability and not for knowledge of correct spelling, because this had been a factor in the initial word selection where homonyms were avoided.

1. I_ wa_ fro_ my D__.   (It was from my Dad)
2. I wi__ s_ip on th_ gra__   (I will slip on the grass)
3. Mu_ cam_ wi__ m_.   (Mum came with me)
4. I d_ n__ lik_ Da_.   (I do not like Dan)
5. A ca_ ca__ t_ the hou__.   (A cat came to the house)

6. I ra_ to the sh__.　　　　　　　(I ran to the shop)
7. I ca_ rid_ m_ bi__.　　　　　　(I can ride my bike)
8. My do_ is i_ the gar___.　　　(My dog is in the garden)

It was noticeable in several cases that the last activity was difficult for the P-type pupils, who rely heavily on the symbols and needed encouragement to hypothesize on such elements as deleted letters.

L-types (using left hand to stimulate right cerebral hemisphere)

1. The pupil evaluates word pairs and decided whether or not they are identical.
2. The pupil palpates and names concrete objects or words and finds a corresponding picture/word on a plate. A decision must be made after palpating the last letter. This is to discourage a hasty and potentially inappropriate response.
3. The pupil palpates a word on the planning board, e.g. 'mat'. At the same time, the words 'map', 'mat' and 'man' are presented visually to the pupil, who must decide which is the same word as the one he or she has palpated. The implications of making a premature decision are discussed and the pupil is made aware of the consequences of making a decision before they are in possession of all the facts about all the possibilities.

For L-types, concrete words, e.g. objects and shapes, should be used as these are considered to rely more heavily on right hemisphere functions than abstract words. Additionally, perceptually complex letter types should be used or a mixture of upper and lower case letters. As far as possible pupils in this group should be discouraged from guessing.

Example of an L-type lesson (early stages)

There now follows a description of a session for an L-type pupil, with limited reading ability. The first two activities are the same as for the P-type pupil, but it can be seen that the words and sentences are more concrete and imageable.

Naming words

1. sink
2. black
3. flat
4. pit
5. mad
6. fat
7. sad
8. cat
9. dad
10. pan

Sentences

When reading the sentences, the L-type pupil is not required to answer questions on serial order but merely reads the sentences aloud.

1. Dad has a fast cat.
2. Dan is in a sandpit.
3. Dad sat on a hat.
4. Pat has a pin.
5. Pat has a big dog.

Same/different

The next activity involves the pupil palpating two words and deciding whether they are the same or different. It can be seen that the words selected are similar and differ in only one or two letters. These may traditionally be the type of words that the L-type may confuse if they respond globally to the word instead of paying attention to the micro elements of the individual letters. Discussion should draw attention to the importance of the individual letters in the words and the difference made by the vowel, for example in the words 'pin' and 'pan'.

1. pin / pan
2. Dad / Dad
3. fat / fast
4. sat / sit
5. nap / nap
6. we / me
7. tip / pit
8. fit / fat
9. Dan / dad
10. is / it

Find the picture

The next activity uses picture stimuli, which again maximizes the greater involvement of the right hemisphere. For this activity the pupil is presented with three or four simple pictures of objects and is required to palpate a word and make a choice as to which of the pictures represents the word. Again, the micro elements of the letters within the words can be used to advantage. For example, for the first word 'hat', the pupil is presented with pictures of a hat, a cat and a bat. They can make an accurate response only if they respond to all the letters and not just the word-ending, which is the same in all cases.

1. hat
2. sun
3. man
4. pan
5. pin
6. dog
7. leg
8. house
9. pen
10. run

Throughout the work, the importance of the actual letters was stressed and the pupil was explicitly reminded to avoid guessing and to check the accuracy of his or her decoding against the evidence he or she was gaining from feeling the actual letters.

The effects of the intervention can be described in terms of both overall results of studies and individual effects for pupils. Three case studies demonstrate the impact of HSS tactile for three pupils, who are part of the sample of the study presented in detail in Chapter 7 (Robertson 1996). This study was a small-sample study involving six pupils only. All had statements of special educational needs for specific learning difficulties and received individual support from a specialist teacher on a weekly basis. In this study the intervention was delivered by the writer and three teachers from a specialist support service. The following case studies may allow differential effects to be observed. The three pupils, who will be discussed in some detail, were all assessed and taught by the author, who was in a position to evaluate fully their response to the technique. Two of the pupils selected for detailed presentation are L-type dyslexic pupils and the differential results obtained following stimulation of the right cerebral hemisphere can be contrasted with the results of the P-type pupil. The outcomes for these pupils demonstrate the importance of individual results. (As with the pupils reported in Chapter 4, all names have been changed to safeguard pupil confidentiality.)

Case study 1: Liam

Liam, a boy of almost 10 years of age, attended a mainstream primary school. He had recently received a statement, which identified him as having specific learning difficulties (the preferred term in his LEA). Prior to the HSS intervention he had been in receipt of individual support for only two months. Under the terms of his statement, he was entitled to three individual sessions of 40 minutes per week. It was decided the HSS approach would be suitable to his needs, as more traditional classroom approaches had been tried throughout his primary school career. His parents were concerned that, as transfer to secondary school was imminent, his need to make progress in reading was urgent. His initial assessment results are found in Table 5.1.

Table 5.1 Pre-intervention testing (Neale Analysis of Reading Ability, NARA) on Liam, 9 years 11 months

Reading age (accuracy)	No score	(raw score 5)
Reading age (comprehension)	5.08 years	(raw score 5)
Rate of reading	No score	(raw score 4)
Substantive errors	38	
Fragmentation errors	6	

To ascertain Liam's baseline reading performance, a Neale Analysis of Reading Ability (NARA) was administered (for results see Table 5.1). Although clearly lacking in confidence towards the reading task, he was co-operative throughout testing. His use of picture clues was marked and he looked at the picture when he could not decipher the text. One noticeable feature was pronounced slow reading. (Passage I of 26 words yielded a time of 102 seconds and Passage 2 of 52 words, 265 seconds.) Liam was ultimately identified as an L-type pupil, so this slow reading was very unusual, as it is more usual for the L-type pupils to demonstrate a faster reading style than average. Reading behaviour showed that words were known by sight or guessed at immediately with no attempt to use word-building or word-attack strategies for unknown words. (Examples included 'pecking' for 'hopped', 'can' for 'gave' and 'about' for 'after'.) Any attempts at unknown words were inconsistent, for example he made two attempts at the word 'her', one being 'make' and the other 'he'. He made 11 attempts to use the initial letter as a word-attack approach, but his lack of success in ultimate decoding showed that, for him, this was not a useful strategy at this particular time or stage of reading development. Lack of comprehension was evident and there were no attempts at self-correction. Despite this, Liam scored 3 for comprehension as he could answer simple literal comprehension questions on the text. His close analysis of the picture accompanying the text was thought to be a possible contributory factor.

When analysed, the errors totalled 30: of which 23 were substitutions, six refusals and one a reversal. When analysed according to the criteria of Bakker, there were a total of 38 substantive errors and six fragmentation errors. This does denote the typically L-type pattern. Of the 38 substantive errors, 23 showed correct adherence to the initial letter, showing this was a powerful determinant for this pupil.

Other difficulties for this pupil included word-finding and retrieval problems and apparent inability to pronounce certain words or even to position the mouth correctly. Phonological ability was limited. There was a pronounced inability to blend words, syllables or letters. Rhyming ability was also found to be deficient.

An additional measure for this pupil was the Boder Test of Reading and Spelling Patterns (Boder and Jarrico 1982) and from this analysis a dysphonetic profile emerged. When computed, the reading age from the Boder Test (single-word reading) was 5.08 years.

As indicated both by the literature and adherence to the developmental model, HSS of the right hemisphere was initiated. It was considered that despite the slow reading speed of this pupil, the main deficit in his reading ability was in reading accuracy rather than reading fluency. It was therefore decided to use stimulation of the right hemisphere. Treatment using the tactile training box took place over 13 sessions using concrete imagery to facilitate visualization and using the left hand to stimulate the right hemisphere.

Liam initially responded positively to the novelty aspect of the tasks and invested considerable effort throughout. He was observed to show the following reading behaviours, commonly associated with the L-type profile. The first was to respond to the word/letter on the basis of minimal information, for example to feel the downstroke of the b', 'd', 'p', 'l' and 'h' and to name the letter. The particular construction of the tactile training box made this clearly visible to the researcher from the side opposite the pupil. The second aspect was that reading tasks were carried out as if he were under time pressure. (This was unusual when contrasted with his originally slow reading of the NARA passages.)

Following the 13-week intervention, Liam was reassessed (Table 5.2). The interval between pre-and post-testing was 7 months. On this occasion of testing, his reading had gained speed and he now read the passage in 52 seconds (previously 102). He was more confident and showed greater fluency in his reading. Notably, he had begun to score on the reading test, and all substitutions now showed accuracy in keeping the first sound constant. A possible interpretation was that he had begun to recognize the perceptual importance of the symbols and had acquired the beginnings of sound/symbol correspondence.

On the simpler first two passages of the NARA, word attempts were still not consistent but were closer to the stimulus word. Analysis of the error pattern revealed seven errors, all word substitutions.

When the NARA was analysed according to the criteria of Bakker, from these two passages there was a total of 22 substantive errors and 10 fragmentation errors. This still denotes the typical L-type pattern but reveals an increase in the fragmentation errors against the pre-testing (six errors only). Of the substantive

Table 5.2 Post-intervention testing (Neale Analysis of Reading Ability, NARA) on Liam, 10 years 6 months

Reading age (accuracy)	5.02 years	(raw score 9)
Reading age (comprehension)	5.06 years	(raw score 4)
Rate of reading	No score	(raw score 10)
Substantive errors	22	
Fragmentation errors	10	

errors, 20 of the 22 showed correct adherence to the initial letter. The reading age according to the Boder Test was now 6.1 years (an increase of 5 months in 13 weeks of treatment). Again the test-retest interval was 7 months and though the rate of improvement was only slightly less than the time interval, it might again be appropriate to question whether a boy who had been a non-reader on the occasion of the first test could be expected to make month-for-month progress on a standardized measure.

Teacher observation (both by the researcher and his mainstream class teacher) confirmed that his reading appeared to have improved. The improvement in standardized scores was minimal but at least the pupil had begun to score on a standardized measure of reading accuracy. Although not reflected in standardized scores, his reading appeared to have gained speed and had become more fluent. Word attempts were consistent and there was evidence of self-corrections (three on this occasion). Although speculative, this could indicate that reading had become a more meaningful activity for this pupil and that he had realized that text signified meaning.

Follow-up testing after 16 weeks revealed what became a common pattern of improved reading test scores even following the 6-week summer holiday (see Table 5.3).

Table 5.3 Follow-up testing (Neale Analysis of Reading Ability, NARA) on Liam, 10 years 10 months

Reading age (accuracy)	5.05years	(raw score 12)
Reading age (comprehension)	5.06 years	(raw score 4)
Rate of reading	No data available	
Substantive errors	25	
Fragmentation errors	9	

Overall the outcomes for this pupil included the following:

- Although improvement in spelling had not been identified as a variable in this study, it was found that independent spelling ability (as revealed by the Boder Test) had improved between the first and second occasions for both known and unknown words. (This has been found in other studies, such as Bakker and Vinke 1985.)
- Reading accuracy had improved according to both the Boder and the NARA measurements. This is supported by the results of other studies, as HSS (tactile) is intended to increase involvement with the right hemisphere, thereby increasing reading accuracy.
- Reading comprehension had almost equivalent results over the three occasions of testing, but observation of the increased self-correction could indicate a more active involvement with the text.

- The number of substantive errors had decreased. This is supported by the theory and could indicate an increased perceptual care to the text. Again, though speculative, according to the Balance Model theory, it could indicate a 'rightening' of hemispheric involvement during reading.
- The number of fragmentation errors had increased marginally and there were attempts to use the indirect route to text, which had previously not been possible for this pupil.
- There was evidence of successful attempts at independent word building.
- Confidence in reading had increased and the pupil was willing to take risks with unknown words.
- The class teacher reported a decrease in behaviour problems within the class-room.
- The boy's parents reported an improvement in attitude to reading and that for the first time he had purchased a book for his own use at home.

Thus for this pupil, there appear to have been some gains in reading accuracy, reading strategies and in the affective area of attitude to reading, which could be attributed to the HSS intervention technique. The extent of the improvement can only be judged partly by analysis of standardized test results and are revealed more effectively when the additional factors of teacher and parent reports are considered. Similar positive outcomes can also be observed by reference to another pupil from the Robertson 1996 study, Karen.

Case study 2: Karen

Karen was classified as having L-type dyslexia. When the intervention began she was 9 years 8 months of age, attended a mainstream primary school and was statemented as having specific learning difficulties. She had been in receipt of support for 2 months only. In the past, all class-based approaches to reading had failed. She was virtually a non-reader with no independent spelling ability. Her self-esteem was severely affected and she required much coaxing to attempt any reading task. Table 5.4 shows Karen's pre-test performance.

Table 5.4 Pre-intervention testing (Neale Analysis of Reading Ability, NARA) on Karen, 9 years 8 months

Reading age (accuracy)	No score
Reading age (comprehension)	No score
Rate of reading	No score
Substantive errors	16
Fragmentation errors	2

The results for this pupil revealed minimal reading ability. She had some metalinguistic (metalanguage being knowledge of the way in which we talk about language, for example knowledge of what constitutes a word or a sentence) strategies and used picture clues to the best of her ability but her lack of reading skill made this ineffective. Words were evidently known by sight or guessed at immediately. There was no evidence of word-building or word-attack strategies. Semantic substitutions were an interesting feature of her reading. Another aspect of interest was that of the nine words read correctly, seven were high-frequency words. This pupil appeared to use the direct route to reading consistently.

During the administration of the Boder Test, Karen was co-operative. She read words systematically and it was clear even at the pre-primer level that words with a phonetically regular pattern did not present her with any advantage. Again, no independent word-building strategies were in evidence. The assessment was for reading only, as the pupil had no independent spelling ability. Classification according to the Boder Test was therefore not possible.

For this pupil there were also word-finding and retrieval problems even to the extent of, on one occasion, describing a gas fire by function rather than name. This was surprising in view of her presenting as an articulate and, superficially, able pupil. There was evidence of inability to pronounce certain (particularly polysyllabic) words or to blend words, syllables or letters.

When a battery of reading subskills was administered, visual perception was adequate until a memory component was added and then sequencing difficulties emerged. In the auditory area, difficulty with discrimination of final sounds was problematic and she had a digit span of four items only. Rhyming ability was deficient. At the affective level, risk-taking was negligible and self-esteem was clearly low.

HSS intervention of the tactile modality was provided according to the developmental model. This utilized concrete imagery to facilitate visualization and involvement with the right hemisphere. As with Liam, there was a positive response to the task and observation again yielded a response to a letter/word on the basis of minimal information. Karen required considerable encouragement to attempt words she could not access immediately and was explicitly instructed to use the feel of the whole letter, in order to attempt to link it to the sound. Both auditory and visual perceptual aspects were stressed for this pupil. Interestingly, within 2 weeks there was a noticeable attempt to access unknown words by sound blending. The intervention continued for 11 weeks and further testing revealed some significant changes in her reading performance (see Table 5.5).

On this occasion, Karen was more confident and showed greater speed and fluency in her reading. Notably, she had now begun to score on the reading test and read the first two sentences with only one error. Substitutions now showed accuracy in keeping the first sound constant and on one occasion the word 'nest' was successfully decoded. Semantic substitutions were no longer a feature of her

Table 5.5 Post-intervention testing (Neale Analysis of Reading Ability, NARA) on Karen, 10 years 2 months

Reading age (accuracy)	5.04years	(raw score 11)
Reading age (comprehension)	6.01 years	(raw score 7)
Rate of reading	No score	
Substantive errors	33	
Fragmentation errors	20	

reading. There was greater comprehension of the text and evidence of self-correction, which could indicate attempts to monitor her reading accuracy. It was noticeable that now 10 of the 16 total errors showed correct grapheme-phoneme correspondence to the first letter. This could indicate an increase in perceptual care or greater confidence in the letter-sound values of certain letters. Substitutions now kept the text meaning intact.

When analysed on the Bakker criteria, there were a total of 33 substantive errors and 20 fragmentation errors. This is a higher error rate than on the first occasion of testing but it had now become appropriate to continue assessment to the more advanced passages. These errors still denote the typically L-type pattern. During administration of the Boder Test, words were read systematically, fluently and confidently. Words with a phonetically regular pattern did not appear to present her with any advantage at the pre-primer level but, surprisingly, did show some advantage at the next reading level. Analysis this time yielded a reading age of 6.2 years. This was a reading age increase of 1.2 years in 5 months on this measure and shows that the reading improvement was not only to be found with the text reading of the NARA but with the single-word reading of the Boder Test.

Spelling this time showed better knowledge of sound/symbol correspondence of the initial letter in all of the words and, despite not fulfilling the strict criteria of the Boder guidelines for selecting good phonetic equivalents (GFEs), there was closer similarity to the stimulus word than prior to the treatment programme. This time the increased spelling ability made classification according to the Boder categories possible, and subsequent analysis yielded a dyseidetic pattern.

This link of the L-type of the Bakker classification and the Boder dyseidetic type is in accordance with the theory, as both subtypes experience difficulty mainly in the visual perceptual field. During testing there was still little attempt to build unknown words with a phonetically regular pattern, despite the increased knowledge of sound/symbol correspondence and the beginning of independent blending ability of three- and four-letter words. This was surprising, as the beginning of independent word-attack strategies was apparent in the intervention sessions. It was noteworthy that the changes were also apparent in spelling ability, which had not been specifically targeted for intervention.

Intervention via the HSS method ceased after 11 sessions. Again, follow-up testing took place after the long summer holiday. The results are shown in Table 5.6.

By this time it was clear that Karen's reading had gained speed and yielded a standardized score for rate of reading for the first time. Overall reading was more confident and fluent. There is now evidence of self-correction and of attempting unknown words, which could indicate that reading had become a more meaningful activity for this pupil. She had now realized that text signified meaning and there were specific strategies one could use to access it. A comprehension score of 10 showed maximum understanding of the meaning of the passages.

Table 5.6 Follow-up testing (Neale Analysis of Reading Ability, NARA) on Karen, 10 years 6 months

Reading age (accuracy)	6.05 years	(raw score 25)
Reading age (comprehension)	6.09 years	(raw score 10)
Rate of reading	5.01 years	(raw score 23)
Substantive errors	11	
Fragmentation errors	9	

She now made clear attempts to access the text by the indirect or phonemic route. Reading had thus progressed to the more competent reading style of modifying the reading approach according to text difficulty. There was evidence of the confidence to take risks with unknown words and the beginnings of successful word-attack strategies. There were indications of either increased perceptual care or greater confidence in the letter-sound values of certain letters. There had been an apparent 'rightening' of hemispheric involvement as demonstrated by the observable reading behaviour.

Analysis according to the Bakker criteria revealed an increase in the fragmentation errors against occasion 1 (two errors only). The fragmentation errors reflect both attempts at independent word-building and self-correction behaviour. Both of these elements were missing in the pupil's original reading strategies, so can indicate a change in the approach to reading.

Analysis of the Boder Test results yielded a reading age of 7.1 years. On this occasion, access to both phonetic and non-phonetic words was equivalent.

Summary of results

- Independent spelling ability had improved between occasions 1 and 2 for both known and unknown words. This would be supported by experimental evidence from other studies.
- Reading accuracy had improved considerably using both the NARA (text reading) and the Boder measurements (single words). This is supported by the literature, as HSS (tactile) is intended to facilitate accurate decoding by specific involvement with the right hemisphere.

- Reading comprehension had increased. Within the literature, there is little evidence on the impact of HSS tactile on reading comprehension, but increased reading accuracy to the text should facilitate greater involvement in the semantic aspect.
- The number of fragmentation errors had increased. This is again supported by results from other studies.
- The number of substantive errors had ultimately decreased. This is supported by the literature and could indicate the presence of increased perceptual care to the text. Although speculative, it could also indicate increased involvement of the right hemisphere during the reading process.
- There were now noticeable and successful attempts at independent word building. This could indicate increased ability to access reading by both the direct and the indirect route, which had previously not been possible for this pupil.
- Confidence in reading had increased and the pupil was willing to take risks with unknown words and to use effective self-correction strategies.
- Reading had increased in speed and fluency and yielded a standardized score for rate of reading by occasion 3. This is not supported by the literature, as HSS (tactile) is intended to increase reading accuracy rather than reading fluency.
- Both Karen's class teacher and her parents commented on the improvement she had made in her reading and spelling performance.

In this case study, the results of the theoretically appropriate intervention would seem to have been positive for this pupil. The HSS intervention approach can be seen to be appropriate for the L-type pupil, whose reading approach is hurried and perceptually careless. The rate of presentation of the HSS material inevitably slows down the pupil's reading so that they have time to access all the perceptual information in the text. They are explicitly encouraged to devote more perceptual care to the reading. The approach therefore suits the perceived educational need of the pupil. In contrast, the P-type pupil, whose reading style is slow and laborious, has not been found to respond so positively to the HSS tactile approach.

Follow-up: 3 years later

Karen was assessed and interviewed three years after the intervention programme. She was, by that time, 13 and a half years old and was in year 9 of secondary education. She was again assessed using the NARA and testing on this occasion revealed that she now had a reading discrepancy against her chronological age of 1 year and 3 months in accuracy and was performing at her age level in reading comprehension. The results of the assessment are shown in Table 5.7.

On this occasion her reading was fluent and there was evidence of confidence with the reading task. Most of the fragmentation errors were self-corrections,

Table 5.7 Long-term follow-up testing (Neale Analysis of Reading Ability, NARA) on Karen, 13 years 6 months

Reading age (accuracy)	12.03 years	(raw score 83)
Reading age (comprehension)	13+ years	(raw score 10)
Rate of reading	Not assessed	
Substantive errors	26	
Fragmentation errors	9	

which demonstrated involvement with the meaning of the passage and that she was monitoring her own reading. She reported that she no longer received any support for specific learning difficulties and that she was enjoying school. It was interesting that as the interview progressed, there was still evidence of word-retrieval difficulties. An example of this occurred when she was explaining which were her favourite subjects, describing 'the one where you change your clothes and run around the field'. She reported few difficulties with text access for the curriculum and had a positive attitude to her secondary education.

This case can demonstrate the potential long-term impact of the intervention for certain pupils. In this instance Karen had not begun to read until she was 10 years old, despite five years in which many teachers had tried various remedial approaches. Following the HSS intervention her reading gained seven years in both reading accuracy and reading comprehension in a period of three years. Karen was still a dyslexic pupil, but had been taught to master the hitherto elusive skills of reading and spelling. Bakker (1990) writes of the HSS method as being one in which pupils learn how to learn, and this case possibly supports this principle.

The final case study is also drawn from the Robertson 1996 study, where the results for the P-type pupils were not so positive, and the contrast in outcome can be seen when the results for Paul, a P-type pupil, are presented.

Case study 3: Paul

Paul was 10 years of age, attended a mainstream primary school and was statemented as having specific learning difficulties. Prior to the intervention he had been in receipt of individual support for only two months. The school had belatedly realized the extent of his reading difficulties. This may have been due in part to a superficial decoding ability, which masked the true extent of his difficulties. It was decided HSS of the tactile medium would be suitable to his needs, as more traditional classroom approaches had obviously failed. Paul was a pupil who showed willingness to take risks with unknown words. The results of testing on the NARA, prior to the intervention are outlined in Table 5.8, and reveal an immediate difference in the number and type of errors than for the two L-type pupils.

Table 5.8 Pre-intervention testing (Neale Analysis of Reading Ability, NARA) on Paul, 10 years

Reading accuracy	5.07 years	(raw score 14)
Reading comprehension	6.06 years	(raw score 9)
Reading rate	No score	
Substantive errors	7	
Fragmentation errors	14	

Initial testing revealed that, although clearly lacking in confidence towards the reading task, the pupil was co-operative throughout testing and was clearly keen to perform to the best of his ability. He frequently asked for reassurance throughout the testing. As the pupil made very few real errors (two only), the level of text difficulty does appear to be at the independent level. One notable feature was pronounced slow reading, which is indicative of P-type dyslexia (passage 1 of 26 words yielded a time of 134 seconds). Slow letter-by-letter decoding was a significant feature of Paul's reading style and indicated use of the indirect route to reading, even for the phonetically irregular words for which it was inappropriate.

Final analysis according to the Bakker criteria yielded seven substantive errors and 14 fragmentation errors. This denotes the typical P-type pattern, which was supported by the exceptionally slow reading style.

During administration of the Boder Test the pupil was again co-operative. Words were read systematically and it was clear even at the pre-primer level that words with a phonetically regular pattern did present Paul with an advantage. Independent word-building strategies were evident, but as these were used for both phonetically regular and irregular words they were not always appropriate.

Spelling generally showed some accurate knowledge of sound/symbol correspondence and a phonetic approach to unknown words. Other errors seemed to indicate inaccurate revisualization of the stimulus word rather than phonetic attempts. Assessment results drew the author to conclude that the pupil was a P-type pupil who yielded a mixed dysphonetic/dyseidetic classification using the Boder categories.

Other difficulties for this pupil included extremely lethargic behaviour, coupled with slow output of work. There was limited motivation to reading and reading-related tasks and it was difficult to find materials he enjoyed. Strengths for this pupil were knowledge of several initial letter/sound values and ability in certain phonological subskills, such as rhyming.

HSS intervention through the tactile modality was provided according to the theory, using the fingers of the right hand. The pupil initially responded positively to the novelty aspect of the task, although his reading, which was usually slow, became even slower. Letters were palpated many times before being named aloud and he seemed reluctant to attempt tasks involving words or sentences with letters omitted. He was obviously lacking in confidence towards the activity and required substantial reassurance from the writer. Motivation was a continuous challenge. Following the HSS intervention, testing gave the results shown in Table 5.9.

Interpretation of the specific error categories was problematic: the pupil had progressed to the next level of text, which, though in line with the NARA administration guidelines, involved an attempt at the next level of reading, and severely challenged this pupil.

On this occasion of testing Paul was more confident and showed greater fluency in his reading, though still accessing both familiar and unfamiliar words by the indirect route. Word attempts were still slowing down the reading considerably and error analysis on the simpler text showed only refusals, all substitutions having been subsequently corrected. Comprehension questions were answered effortlessly.

As the text increased in difficulty, reading slowed and the pupil continued the laborious task of letter-by-letter decoding. This strategy, although still evident, had decreased (now six times as opposed to the original 10) but was still successful only with the word 'had'. NARA error analysis here revealed a slightly different profile to the first occasion of testing. Of the 14 errors, five were substitutions, eight were refusals, either on sight or following an initial attempt at word building, and there was one visuospatial reversal. This reversal, along with the increase in the number of substitutions, could indicate an attempt to use the direct route to text as opposed to the previously totally predominant indirect route. Comprehension on this occasion scored only 4 as opposed to 6 on occasion 1, with a reduction of two months on a standardized score. Testing was continued for this pupil, who had not reached the ceiling level of errors for this instrument. From the second sentence it was clear the material at the next graded passage level was at frustration level. This resulted (for this passage only) in 15 substitutions, 11 refusals and two omissions. It may be significant that attempts at word building were again very overt and, despite the failure he was experiencing, he did not express any desire for testing to cease. Errors were now occurring on almost every word, and by the third sentence were rarely in keeping with the meaning of the text.

Table 5.9 Post-intervention testing (Neale Analysis of Reading Ability, NARA) on Paul, 10 years 6 months

Reading accuracy	5.09 years	(raw score 14)
Reading comprehension	6.04 years	(raw score 9)
Reading rate	No score	
Substantive errors	40*	
Fragmentation errors	47*	

*Denotes that the pupil had progressed to the next level of text difficulty.

When the NARA was analysed according to the Bakker criteria, from the first two passages there were a total of 19 substantive errors and 22 fragmentation errors. Separate analysis of passage 3 yielded 21 substantive errors and 25 fragmentation errors. This denotes a more mixed profile, which does raise questions regarding the level at which testing is discontinued in this instrument. Pupil behaviour by passage 3 showed a more rapid response to certain words, which could indicate that the pupil had lost motivation in the test and was trying to complete it as quickly as possible, which seems understandable in the face of the failure he was experiencing. Again, the Boder Test was administered to ascertain any differences that could be revealed by single-word reading as opposed to reading connected text. During administration of this test, words were read systematically and there was a more equivalent response to regular and irregular words. Although not measured, reading appeared to have gained fluency. Spelling results again yielded a mixed profile. The pupil was assessed 16 weeks following intervention and certain differences were found. The extent of these was revealed when a qualitative analysis of his reading was carried out in addition to the changes in standardized scores (Table 5.10).

An important element was that his reading had gained speed and on this occasion the reading of the first passage was achieved in 45 seconds (previously 102). Paul was more confident and showed greater fluency in his reading. There was now less evidence of the tendency to access both known and unknown words by the indirect route for reading. Notably this was now used, albeit successfully, on only one occasion. Refusals were more immediate and were rarely prefaced by laborious decoding. There was an increase in the number of semantically appropriate substitutions (six substitutions and two self-corrections), which could indicate an attempt to use the direct route to text, as opposed to the previously totally predominant indirect route of pre-testing.

Throughout the HSS intervention, motivation was a continual problem with this pupil. Lack of motivation was not found only with the HSS material but was also evident in all written work, both in the classroom and in the individual support sessions. Throughout it had been difficult to find any material the pupil enjoyed. The results showed that for this pupil, although overall gains in the various measures were not so evident, there were some changes in reading profile.

Table 5.10 Follow-up testing (Neale Analysis of Reading Ability, NARA) on Paul, 10 years 10 months

Reading accuracy	5.11 years	(raw score 18)
Reading comprehension	7.02 years	(raw score 12)
Reading rate	No score	
Substantive errors	14	
Fragmentation errors	8	

These are not so much in overall results but in the style of his reading and were supported by discussions on his classroom performance in reading.

By occasion 3 analysis of the NARA, according to the Bakker criteria, yielded a total of 14 substantive and eight fragmentation errors. This is different from the initial profile and could denote a changed approach to text. During administration of the Boder Test it was no longer so apparent that words with a phonetically regular pattern presented Paul with any advantage, as the results for both phonetic and non-phonetic words were similar. Independent word-building strategies were no longer so much in evidence and reading appeared more fluent.

Summary of results

Overall fluency and rate of reading for this pupil had increased over the 10 months of the study to the extent where he was obtaining a standardized score for rate of reading, but this was not at a sufficient level to obtain a rate of reading age. This is supported by the literature, as HSS (tactile) for P-type pupils is intended to increase semantic and syntactic involvement with the text. (In other studies this has been found to contribute to increased fluency of reading style.)

- Reading accuracy had increased by only four months in the 10-month period between pre- and follow-up testing. This minimal increase is supported by the literature, as P-type intervention is not intended to impact on reading accuracy but rather on fluency of reading.
- Comprehension had gained a total of eight months over testing, with questions being answered more confidently. There is no evidence from the literature on the impact of P-type tactile intervention on reading comprehension. It could be expected, however, that a decrease of spelling-like reading would improve the level of semantic involvement with the text.
- The pupil's approach to text had changed from a predominantly indirect route to reading, to a more direct route, as evidenced by the number of substantive versus fragmentation errors. This is supported by the literature (Bakker 1990), which describes such changes following left-hemisphere HSS (tactile) treatment for P-type pupils.

In the three reported cases, results of the theoretically appropriate intervention would seem to have had positive, though differential, impact. This was observed in the varied aspects of reading behaviour. The changes were revealed not only by alteration in reading test scores on the various measures but also by observation of pupil behaviour during the reading process and discussion with the teachers of the pupils and the pupils themselves.

General discussion of results

The Robertson 1996 study revealed some interesting differences between the different subtypes of Boder and of Bakker. When similarities between the subtype categories of Boder (1973) and Bakker (1990) are made, direct one-to-one correspondences are lacking.

The key is that the L-type's dominant hemisphere is actually a weakness, as it results from an over-reliance on linguistic strategies to access text. Errors derive from inaccurate visual perception and are omissions of letters and words; in short, all 'real' errors. The P-types show the reverse pattern as they, to some extent, are fixated at, and overuse, the right hemisphere (perceptual) strategies, as evidenced by the slow, spelling-like reading. This inappropriate use is in fact a weakness and can be equated with the Boder dysphonetic category.

In this study, the L-type pupils who received HSS (by the tactile medium of the left hand, therefore directed to the right hemisphere) made gains in reading accuracy. Conversely, the P-type pupil given HSS (tactile) directed to the left hemisphere gained in reading fluency but gained little in reading accuracy.

These positive results could help to validate both the L and P classification system and the theoretical basis of the intervention. Results showed that there had been educationally significant benefits for two of the pupils, indicating an increased analytical approach to text, which could herald the beginning of access to word-attack strategies for the L-type pupil. The previously overused analytical approach had declined for the P-type pupil and reading fluency had consequently improved.

One element, which could have contributed to the success for the L-type pupils, is that the speed of text processing had been reduced; HSS by the tactile modality requires the palpation of individual letters. This reduction of speed necessary for accurate perception could increase the potential for perceptual attention, which would be desirable for L-type pupils. Some of the research mentioned previously indicates that dyslexic subjects are weak when processing either visual or auditory stimuli rapidly (Galaburda and Livingstone 1993; Holmes 1994; Rennie 1991; Nicholson and Fawcett 1994; Lehmkuhle et al. 1993; Tallal 1997; Stein 1997; Stein and Walsh 1997). The increased time for processing may therefore have been a powerful contributor to the results. HSS tactile decreases the speed of processing time. (In contrast, HSS delivered via the visual half-field increases the processing time but equally has been found to reveal positive results for some pupils.)

Conclusions

It must be admitted that the delivery of HSS intervention is time-consuming and involves much initial preparation on the part of the teacher. This may be offset against the improvement in results for certain pupils.

HSS visual involves the selection of words for reading, programming them into the computer and sitting by the pupil so that maximum diagnostic information can be gained. The computer stores the overall results of the sessions, but the teacher can obtain valuable diagnostic information by observation of the pupil performance and discussion following the task.

HSS tactile involves the teacher assembling every word the pupil will decode on a letter-by-letter basis. For a pupil who has significant difficulties with reading, the number of words is considerable over the period of a 40-minute lesson. Yet the results of the Robertson 1996 study, from which the case studies were taken, do support the intervention for those pupils who are experiencing entrenched reading difficulty and so both teacher and pupil are more than rewarded for their efforts. The case study data presented may have served to highlight this point and to demonstrate that, on an individual level, the gains for certain pupils may be substantial, although examination of their individual profiles may reveal improvements in different aspects of the reading process.

Chapter 6
Experimental work from studies into HAS

Introduction

The investigations reported in this chapter present the results of studies using hemisphere-alluding stimulation as an intervention technique. Both large- and small-scale studies have been carried out and the results of some of these are presented. The HAS studies are generally from the Netherlands but one is also reported on a UK sample.

An investigation was reported on a large-scale study in the Netherlands (Bakker 1990), involving 60 remedial teachers and 90 pupils. The design of this study involved both P-type and L-type subtypes and P-type and L-type control groups. The results demonstrated that after intervention, the L-type dyslexic pupils showed improvement in sentence reading accuracy. They also made less substantive errors than the L-type control subjects. In contrast, the P-type dyslexic pupils showed greater improvements in their fluency of single-word reading, as demonstrated by the number of fragmentation errors made.

Results of experimental work in the UK (Robertson 1996)

The sample for this study was selected from pupils within three LEAs and all were statemented under the Code of Practice for the identification and assessment of pupils with special educational needs (DES 1994). All were pupils who attended mainstream primary and secondary schools. They had all been in receipt of support, via multisensory teaching methods, over periods of time ranging from six months to three years. In all cases the support was delivered by specialist teachers, and individual provision was made by withdrawing the pupils from mainstream lessons for periods of time ranging from 40 minutes to one hour.

The study took place over a period of 12 weeks on a sample of 37 pupils aged between 7 and 13 years. The pupils were from three LEAs and involved the author (as one of the providers of the teaching) and 15 teachers, who had volunteered to take part. All the pupils were already receiving individual support so this could compensate for any Hawthorne Effects, which might otherwise have impacted on results. (Hawthorne Effects are effects on subjects, derived mainly from the experience of being, in this case, the recipient of focused individual attention).

Prior to intervention, the pupils were tested using the Neale Analysis of Reading Ability (NARA) (Neale 1989). This was selected as it would allow reading to be analysed for rate and comprehension, in addition to reading accuracy. This could allow other differences in reading behaviour to be revealed and analysed. As the NARA is based on graded passages of text in context, it can also be used as a basis for the adapted miscue analysis procedure devised by Bakker. Following initial testing it was intended to classify pupils into the two categories of L- and P-type. When the results were analysed this was not possible, as of the 37 pupils in the sample, 21 made almost equivalent numbers of substantive and fragmentation errors. Upon further analysis, there was evidence of a group who made errors of both types and who could form the basis of yet another subtype. The experimental design was subsequently adapted to investigate whether the results of this group showed qualitatively different responses to intervention to the pure L- and P-type pupils. This allowed the validity of both the classification and the theory to be examined. There was also an attempt to discover if teaching should be aimed at the strongest or the weakest modality, as a challenge study was proposed to evaluate if differentiated intervention was supported. It was considered that this could be justified ethically, as an ongoing debate in the provision of specialist teaching has been whether teaching should be aimed at the strongest or the weakest modality. Opinions vary, but examples of both theoretical positions can be found when a range of intervention techniques are examined.

Following initial assessment of the sample, pupils were classified as L-type, P-type (one pupil only) or M-type (mixed). This was unexpected in view of the Bakker categorization, which had shown that, in the studies in the Netherlands, the P-type was the largest group. This may reflect differences in the identification and assessment arrangements between the UK and the Netherlands. As the sample was taken from pupils statemented as having specific learning difficulties, this may involve more pupils having problems of reading accuracy, which depress test scores. Under the arrangements in the UK, in order to obtain a statement of special educational need, there is usually a decrement of reading age when compared to chronological age. The P-type pupil, whose reading behaviour is slow and marked by explicit phoneme-grapheme correspondence, but who may ultimately decode the word correctly, may not be recognized as readily by this criterion. His superficial reading skill of being able to decode words successfully may also mask the extent of the difficulties, so may be under-represented in a statemented sample.

The final design was amended to reflect the subtype categorization and thus became two categories only – L-type and M-type pupils. These were randomly assigned to groups in order to receive intervention by either P-type materials, which theoretically alluded more to left hemisphere semantic processes, or by L-type materials, which theoretically alluded more to the right hemisphere processes, by their visuo-perceptual emphasis (see Figure 6.1). It was hoped that differential pupil results could validate differential intervention. This would be particularly revealing in the case of the newly identified M-type group.

L-type pupils given P-type materials (LP)
L-type pupils given L-type materials (LL)
M-type pupils given L-type materials (ML)
M-type pupils given P-type materials (MP)

Figure 6.1 Amended research design.

The intervention

All pupils received intervention, once weekly over a period of 13 weeks. The sessions involved approximately 25 minutes reading modified text and 15 minutes using textually provided exercises to stimulate the intended cerebral hemisphere. The author provided all the reading material and exercises to allow for consistency. The reading material given to the pupils was age, reading-ability and as far as possible, interest-level appropriate, although this was difficult for older pupils in the sample who had reading accuracy ages less than 7 years. All the textual modifications complied with the specifications of Bakker (1990) and were confirmed by him as being appropriate.

Teacher response to the intervention

The teachers were enthusiastic about the intervention, although some expressed concern that a whole teaching session was devoted to reading only and that no spelling work was undertaken as part of the sessions. They were also concerned that if the pupil was using the P-type materials, no illustrations were included (as they would have alluded more to the right hemisphere) and that made the text more difficult for the pupil to decode. All the teachers were trained as to the appropriate response, depending on the material they were using. The teachers using the L-type materials with pupils were told to stress accuracy of decoding and to urge the pupils to look carefully at the text before committing themselves to a final decision. In contrast, the teachers using the P-type materials with pupils stressed speed of response and when the pupil encountered a space (occasioned by a deleted word) they were encouraged to find a word which fitted into the context as quickly as possible.

Some teachers also expressed concern that some of the exercises seemed difficult for the pupils. As the work progressed, many commented that certain of the
exercises were carried out more proficiently by the pupils than the teachers! There
was an appreciation that the range of exercises devised provided a variety of tasks
and so helped to maintain pupil motivation, particularly after a considerable
amount of time spent reading the adapted text.

Pupil response to the intervention

The pupils were all prepared for the appearance of the text by the teachers and were
informed that it was to help them specifically with their reading. As the intervention
proceeded, some pupils required encouragement to persevere as they found the text
challenging (despite it being age- and reading age-appropriate). The teachers had all
been informed that the overriding consideration was the feelings of the pupils and
that if any showed signs of stress or lack of motivation, then the work should be
terminated. This was carried out with one pupil after four intervention sessions only.
Subsequent discussion with the teacher and scrutiny of his results showed he had
been the sample's only P-type pupil, and had been provided with materials to stimulate the right hemisphere (due to the challenge design of the study). In real terms, this
means that a pupil for whom reading was over-concentrated on the perceptual
aspects had been provided with materials designed to make the task more perceptually challenging and to slow the process down. The pupil therefore (quite justifi-
ably) became the only pupil to refuse to proceed with the work.

Results after intervention

The main areas of interest had been defined as:

- reading accuracy
- reading comprehension
- reading rate
- number of substantive (real) errors
- number of fragmentation (time-consuming) errors.

HAS: clinical observations

Results on differential pupil X group interventions on the various factors of
interest can be summarized as follows:

Reading accuracy

L-type pupils matched with L-type materials (LL group) all improved in reading
accuracy (from 1 year 7 months to 1 year 11 months), whereas L-type pupils
matched with P-type materials (LP group) did not.

Reading comprehension

Pupils from both LP and LL groups gained in reading comprehension and for the LL group the improvement in comprehension was in excess of two and a half years for each pupil. The substantial increase in comprehension for the LP group was not surprising. (P-type materials encourage semantic and syntactic interaction with the text.)

Error analysis

The LL group showed variable increases in the number of both substantive and fragmentation errors but overall accuracy still increased. This could reflect the scoring criteria of the NARA, as most fragmentation errors would not count as errors, unlike substantive errors, which would be reflected in the scoring.

Discussion of results

The result of this study yielded some evidence of type X treatment interactions. The pupils in the LL group showed an improvement in reading accuracy, whereas those in the LP group did not. Error analysis for these pupils may reflect a more analytic approach to text and could indicate the beginning of independent word-attack strategies. On an individual case study level, the results for certain pupils were considerable, as described in Chapter 4.

Validity of the classification

These positive results could help to validate both the L and P classification systems and the theoretical basis of the intervention. Results indicated that there had been educationally significant results for certain of the pupils, with an increased analytical approach to text, which could herald the beginning of access to word-attack strategies. Results in this study are hemisphere-specific, as stimulation of the right hemisphere generally improved reading accuracy. This would be consistent with the Novelty theory of Goldberg and Costa (1981), whereby the right hemisphere is more effective in processing novelty stimuli. It is also consistent with theories of hemisphere-specific activation and reciprocal balance (Kinsbourne 1989). The right hemisphere is primed by the nature of the tasks to enable effective processing of text to take place. This would not be so for the readers treated with the P-type materials. Here, the hemisphere primed (the left hemisphere) would not be best suited to the initial reading (mainly involving the right hemisphere) so that the reciprocal balance between hemisphere and task could not be achieved.

Post-intervention results

Kappers (1997) wrote of certain 'factors beyond the method' possibly being in evidence, as even after intervention had ceased the LL pupils continued to make reading gains. This could indicate that a change of hemispheric involvement had taken place, as relapses in performance following holidays are well observed phenomena for those supporting pupils with reading difficulties. The results were also viewed positively as many involved follow-up testing immediately following the six-week summer vacation. At this time it could realistically be assumed that pupils had not been in such regular contact with written text as they had been during the school term. This could be seen as an important validation of the teaching approach as teachers often report retention of improvements or even regression as being a considerable problem after even short school holidays.

Another interesting perspective from the teachers concerned the prepared materials. Upon completion of the study, several teachers retained them for use with other pupils and used them as supplementary materials on a regular basis. They reported improvements in certain aspects of the reading process by using only the prepared exercises in the absence of adapted texts. (The evidence here was derived from teacher perceptions only and was not validated by formal assessment.)

Comparison with other studies

When comparisons are made between studies, results clearly vary. Other workers have noted this and Bakker (1994) observed that in addition to differences in subtype and hemisphere, effects may be investigation-specific in that L-types may react better in one study and P-types in another. Some experimental effects may also be skill-specific, as in some studies comprehension improved but naming did not (Russo 1993), whereas other differences may be child-specific, as individual treatment effects vary. Results may range from those subjects showing little or no improvement to those who seem completely 'cured' (Kappers and Hamburger 1994).

Results vary between studies, and certain factors need to be addressed. Included here would be classification methods, as L-types in one study would not necessarily be L-types in another study. They may not be L-types following the intervention but this may be an indication that the approach to text has changed in the desired direction. This does, however, render the provision of differential inter-vention problematic. Also pertinent is the role of phonology: the Balance Model sees phonological skill as a right hemisphere activity with the emphasis on the initial visual analysis and automaticity aspect of the grapheme–phoneme conver-sion. The auditory processing aspect of phonology is not disputed as being a predominantly left hemisphere process, but the initial visual analysis of the individual grapheme concerns spatial awareness, which involves the right hemisphere to a larger extent.

Conclusion

Results from the study reported here should be interpreted cautiously, as sample numbers were small and pupils received a small number of treatment sessions. Yet there did seem to be a change of response to text by the pupils.

In conclusion, these small-scale studies show that HAS intervention can be effective in increasing the reading skill of certain pupils with reading difficulties. Results suggest that HAS can allow certain aptitude X instruction interactions (AIIs) (Pumfrey and Reason 1991) of utility to be identified. It may prove to be an alternative treatment method, by which pupil reading strengths and weaknesses benefit from differentiated intervention through more individually designed programmes.

One element that could have contributed is that both treatment methods reduce the speed of text processing for the L-type subjects; HAS by deliberate modification of the text and HSS (tactile modality) requiring the palpation of individual letters. This reduction of speed could increase the potential for perceptual attention and could be supported by the research, which indicates that dyslexic subjects are weak when processing either visual or auditory stimuli rapidly (McNally and Stein 1996; Tallal et al. 1996; Talcott et al. 1997).

Chapter 7
Experimental work from HSS studies

Introduction

All studies in this section concern intervention via either the tactile receptors of the hands or via the visual half-fields using the previously discussed computer program HEMSTIM. Both can be adapted to allow for stimulation of either the left or the right cerebral hemisphere, depending on the theoretical-based needs of the pupil. The results are presented in terms of main effects on pupils.

Small-scale UK study (Robertson 1996)

The sample for this study comprised pupils from two LEAs, all of whom were in receipt of statements as having specific learning difficulties. They were all receiving support from specialist teachers and ranged in age from 9 to 14 years. An additional criterion for this group was that of persistent reading difficulty, as all pupils had deficits of reading accuracy over chronological age greater than four years. In the case of one pupil, with virtually no independent reading ability, it was necessary to teach her to read five words before the intervention could be delivered. The entrenched reading difficulties of pupils in this group rendered a challenge design inappropriate. All pupils were given intervention according to the theory and in the case of one virtual non-reader and one M-type pupil, intervention was given according to the developmental model. This meant that stimulation began with the right hemisphere.

The NARA was used as both a classification instrument and a measure by which pupil progress in reading accuracy, reading comprehension and rate of reading could be calculated. The graded text passages also provided a means of assessing pupil-reading errors according to the criteria of Bakker (1990) and it was hoped this would allow changes in reading behaviour to be identified and measured.

To maintain uniformity, the author provided all teaching materials and teachers were trained in the appropriate response for both subtypes of pupils. In the case of the P-types, fluency was stressed, whereas for the L-types, accuracy was the main criterion. All materials given to the pupils were age-, reading age- and as far as possible, interest level-appropriate, although this again was difficult in the case of older pupils with severely depressed reading accuracy ages.

Teacher response to the intervention

Before delivering the intervention, the teachers were provided with lesson plans for the duration of the study and were asked to make notes about pupils' responses to the material. Their reports were favourable despite the time-consuming preparation for the individual sessions.

Pupil response to the intervention

The pupils were given one introductory session to familiarize them with the technique and allow them to acquaint themselves with the notion of reading using their fingertips rather than via the more usual visual channel. The importance of using a specified hand was stressed. All teachers reported initially favourable responses to the approach.

The study into the effects of HSS tactile was undertaken on six pupils over a period of up to 13 weeks and the results on the main factors of interest are presented below.

Reading accuracy

Reading accuracy on the NARA improved over all occasions for all pupils. It is noteworthy that for three pupils this was the first occasion they had achieved a measurable reading accuracy age on a standardized reading test. Previously their scores had been below the level at which an age equivalent could be found on the standardized form of this measure. Clinically, beginning to score is significant as all of the pupils in this sample had experienced entrenched reading failure, despite receiving individual specialist support on a weekly basis, lasting for between two months and three years.

Reading comprehension

Reading comprehension scores (NARA) showed gains for five of the six pupils. As with reading accuracy, two pupils achieved reading comprehension ages for the first time. Although results varied, gains for three pupils were in excess of one year. Increases in reading comprehension would be expected if reading accuracy improved, but it may also signal greater and more active involvement in the reading process.

Changes in error performance

The number of substantive (real) errors showed variability with reductions for the L-type pupils but not for the P- or the M-types. This is a predicted type X treatment effect and could demonstrate that the pupils had begun to pay more perceptual care to the symbols of the reading process. The L-type materials are also designed to improve reading accuracy, so if the theory were supported, the number of real errors would decrease correspondingly.

The number of fragmentation errors showed variability, but five of the six pupils (including the L-type pupils) showed a substantial increase between occasions 1 and 2. This may again indicate a type X treatment effect. In the case of the L-type pupils, an increase of the fragmentation error could signal use of explicit decoding and the ability to access text by the indirect (phonemic analysis) as well as by the direct route.

As in experimental evidence from the previously reported HAS study (Robertson 1996), the results for individuals varied. Group effects can present only part of the picture in intervention studies, as the results for certain individuals were educationally significant and have been presented in detail in Chapter 5.

Results of one UK study using HSS (computer)

This study took place on secondary school pupils, who were all receiving individual support for their literacy difficulties (Johnson and Robertson 1999). The sample comprised 20 pupils, who were each assessed on the NARA and randomly allocated to HEMSTIM intervention. They were all given HSS treatment first directed at one hemisphere, they were then retested and given HEMSTIM treatment of the other hemisphere. Random allocation was considered ethically justified, as the literature fails to provide support for directing teaching at either the strongest or the weakest modality. Some teachers advocate teaching to strengths while others advocate attempting to remediate deficiencies in the weakest medium. The evidence seems to be inconclusive, although clearly the pupil must be presented with materials which maximize the possibility of success. This experimental study involved HEMSTIM treatment for 10 weeks, retesting and then subsequent teaching, again for 10 weeks. The results were interesting and revealed considerable increases in the varied measures of accuracy, comprehension and rate of reading. Patterns were revealed in terms of the type of intervention pupils were given for the initial treatment.

First intervention period

L-type materials for first phase (n = 3)

All pupils gained in reading accuracy between occasions 1 and 2 in a range from 1 year 3 months to 4 years 2 months. This may indicate educationally significant improvements, which were gained over an intervention period of only 10 weeks. This effect is supported by the literature.

Reading comprehension increases for these pupils ranged from 2 years to 3 years 4 months + (pupil reached the ceiling level of the measurement instrument). This is supported by the literature but would also be expected, for if access to the text improved, access to text meaning should improve accordingly. Results for rate of reading were varied; two pupils decreased, one by 2 years 3 months + (originally at ceiling level) and the other by 1 year 3 months. This decrease of reading speed is a desirable outcome and again is supported by the literature as L-type materials are designed to encourage perceptual care. Conversely, one pupil increased in reading speed by 9 months, which is supported by the literature.

P-type materials for phase one (n = 3)

Again, pupils showed gains in reading accuracy in the range of 1 year 2 months to 2 years. This is not supported by the literature, as P-type materials are designed to increase reading speed and fluency rather than reading accuracy. It can be seen that the gains are not as substantial as for the pupils who initially received the L-type materials.

Reading comprehension increases for these pupils were in the range 9 months to 2 years 3 months. This is tentatively supported by the literature, as improved fluency and accuracy of decoding will impact positively on text comprehension. It is noteworthy that, for this group, the increases in rate of reading were consistent (unlike those treated with the L-type materials) and were almost identical in that they were 1 year 8 months, 1 year 9 months and 1 year 10 months respectively.

Second intervention period

P-type materials (n = 3)

The results for this experimental period reveal a different pattern. Two of the three pupils decreased in reading accuracy by 10 months and one gained by only 3 months. This could again be supported by the literature as P-type materials are designed to impact on reading fluency rather than accuracy.

Comprehension scores also reflect similar individual differences; one pupil gained 1 year 1 month, one stayed the same (interpretation is difficult as the ceiling level of the test was reached) and one decreased in reading comprehension by 2 years and 1 month. Interpretation for rate of reading is inconsistent; one pupil decreased by 1 month, one increased by 1 year 4 months and for one pupil data were unavailable.

L-type materials (n = 3)

Results for reading accuracy varied for this group; one pupil decreased by 7 months while the other pupils gained 1 year 2 months and 1 year 6 months respectively.

Reading comprehension results also varied as the pupil who had decreased in reading accuracy also decreased in reading comprehension by 2 years 3 months, while the other two gained by 11 months + (ceiling level impact) and 1 year 7 months respectively. Results for rate of reading were more consistent; one pupil gained 1 month but the other two decreased by 2 months and 9 months respectively. Though these results are slight, they are nevertheless in the expected direction as the L-type materials are designed to increase perceptual attention, which has the effect of reducing reading speed and here seem to be reflected in the standardized scores for rate of reading.

Discussion

Overall results vary but do show some subtype X treatment interactions.

- Pupils treated with the L-type materials made greater gains in reading accuracy during the period when they received stimulation of the right hemisphere.
- Pupils treated with the P-type materials showed more consistent increases in score for rate of reading. Conversely, pupils treated with the L-type materials showed a more consistent decrease in rate of reading during the period they received the right hemisphere stimulation.

The trend of these results does seem to support the differentiated outcomes of the intervention. Overall results vary but, with the exception of one pupil, all gained in reading accuracy over the 20 weeks of the intervention. Some pupils made more significant gains than others, but when it is considered that the pupils were all statemented as having specific learning difficulties and had decrements of reading age over chronological age in a range from 5 years to 9 years, the results are promising. The sample comprised secondary school-aged pupils with entrenched difficulties of text access. For such pupils it may be unrealistic to expect a month for month increase in standardized reading scores but for many pupils in the sample the increases were far in excess of this. An interesting result of this study was that the classification theory was not supported. Individual treatment effects supported the intervention theory, but did not support the expected trend from the subtype theory. Results were found to be treatment-specific rather than subtype-specific. Thus, pupils given intervention of the right hemisphere (regardless of whether they were L-types) improved in reading accuracy. In contrast, those given intervention of the left hemisphere generally improved in reading fluency. This could have implications for classification, and further study is currently being planned to validate these assumptions.

The results of these small-scale studies tentatively support the use of HSS (visual) as a suitable intervention method for dyslexic pupils with difficulties in the varied aspects of textual access. Ongoing research is still required to refine core concepts, such as classification and allocation to subtype, yet pursuit of this may seem to be warranted by the results of the studies presented. Experimental evidence can also be found in studies reported from outside the UK.

Bakker et al. (1990), in a large-scale study on 100 L-type, P-type or matched control group children, found that HSS-treated, L-type dyslexic pupils showed larger improvements in accuracy of text reading, relative to controls, and HSS-treated, P-type dyslexic children showed larger improvement in the fluency of word-reading. One aspect, which differed greatly from the Robertson 1996 study, was that the results for the P-type pupils treated by HSS intervention were more positive. They concluded that the slow information processing required by HSS tactile was better suited to the slow reading style of the P-type as opposed to the rapid processing of words required for HSS delivered via the visual half-fields. Another interesting result of this study was that reading accuracy for the L-types improved only for text reading and that reading fluency for the P-types improved only for word reading. Although speculative, the authors considered that context may stimulate the guessing of words, which is the preferred reading strategy of the L-types. Text reading is more suited to this approach so that possibly if a new (right hemisphere) strategy is added, this comes into operation. Conversely, the P-type pupils are relatively insensitive to the contextual information from the text, but are sensitive to perceptual features. Thus, single-word reading is more suited to this reading style and when it is affected by a new (left hemisphere) strategy may demonstrate the impact more effectively.

Other differences found between the groups were revealed when pharmacological intervention was studied. This involved the drug Piracetam (a nootropic drug reported to facilitate reading, specifically speed of reading). (Nootropic drugs are specifically related to mental functioning and the drug Piracetam was the first one to be developed.) Experimentally the drug has been found to stimulate the left hemisphere. Two case studies confirmed that for P-type subjects, a combination of Piracetam and HSS induced faster reading and reduced the frequency of time-consuming errors. Though pharmacological intervention is thankfully not an option for intervention with dyslexic subjects, this report does again demonstrate certain differences between the two groups.

Occasionally other factors may be presumed to impact on the results of studies and this can he highlighted by reference to the following example. Grace and Spreen (1994) conducted a pilot study, followed by a main study, into the effects of HSS visual on L-type subjects. The results varied: the pilot study found the improvements expected by the trend of the literature, whereas the main study did not. Unexpectedly, the L-type subjects decreased in reading accuracy. This led to detailed analysis and it was found that, when the materials used were examined, they included certain symbols, such as '%' and &, which are capable of being coded verbally, so may have induced left hemisphere as opposed to the desired right hemisphere activity.

Neuvonen et al. (1992) carried out multiple single-case studies of dyslexic Finnish-speaking children. They found that all the children who had received the HSS intervention had improved more, on all measures of reading ability, than any of the control children. Dryer et al. (1999), however, in her study in New Zealand found that HSS treatment was not supported by the experimental results. Here the results are difficult to analyse as HAS and HSS were used consecutively on the subjects, which makes the impact of either technique difficult to evaluate.

When comparisons are made between studies, results clearly vary. This has been noted by other workers, and Bakker (1994) notes that in addition to differences in subtype and hemisphere, effects may be investigation-specific in that L-types may react better in one study and P-types in another. Some experimental effects may also be skill-specific (in some studies comprehension improved, though naming did not; Russo 1993), whereas other differences may be child-specific as individual treatment effects vary. The results for individuals range from those subjects showing little or no improvement to those who seem completely 'cured' (Kappers and Hamburger 1994).

Results show clear variation between studies and it would be useful to address certain factors in future work. Included here would be the issue of classification methods, as L-types in one study would not necessarily be L-types in another, which renders both comparison between studies and differential intervention problematic. The role of phonology with regard to the Balance Model is also controversial: the Balance Model sees phonological skill as a right hemisphere activity with the emphasis on the initial visual analysis of the symbol. In contrast, other workers, by stressing the phonemic analysis, equate phonology with a primarily left hemisphere linguistic activity.

An interesting extension of the HSS work in the Netherlands was in a clinical pilot study to evaluate the bilingual effects of neuropsychological intervention (Kappers and Dekker 1995). This derived from studies on the neuropsychological implications of second language learning. These have suggested that the involvement of the right hemisphere will be stronger in the initial stages of learning to read a new language and demonstrates a learning-to-read effect, as opposed to a specific learning-a-second-language effect (Galloway 1982). Other studies have found a shift of visual field preference for English words in native Hebrew speakers (Silverberg et al. 1979, 1980). The Kappers and Dekker work used a combination of HSS tactile and HSS visual on a sample of 14 students, who were all 14 years old and had a long history of dyslexia. All the subjects were assessed on both word and text reading in both languages. An interesting finding was that the results were similar, regardless of the language in which the intervention was delivered (either Dutch or English). Overall, right hemisphere stimulation led to more accurate reading (with fewer substantive errors), but in this study there were unexpected improvements in reading speed. When the overall results were compared, there were higher levels of reading in both Dutch and English text reading but only in

English single-word reading. The authors concluded that short-term treatment in one language might enhance reading in a second, untreated language. This work is interesting, as again there is a record of transfer of learning from one context to another, which had been recorded in other studies.

Conclusions

Results from the studies reported here should be interpreted cautiously, as sample numbers were limited and pupils received a small number of treatment sessions. Yet despite this there did seem to be a change of pupil response to text, according to the intervention method used. In the clinical study, there was a noticeable difference in performance, demonstrating an increase in phonological skill, which impacted on both reading and spelling.

In conclusion, these small-scale studies show that HSS (tactile) intervention can be effective in increasing the reading skill of certain dyslexic pupils with entrenched reading difficulties. Results suggest that HSS can allow certain useful AIIs to be identified. It may prove to be an alternative treatment method by which pupil reading strengths and weaknesses can be addressed by differentiated intervention, leading to more individually tailored programmes. Individual variation in response is great, but it may be possible to reveal factors that are linked to successful outcomes by further study, so that pupils for whom this approach will be successful can be identified.

Chapter 8
Implications of neuropsychological intervention in the treatment of dyslexia

This chapter addresses issues that relate directly to both practical and theoretical considerations. These include:

- the role of phonology in the Balance Model
- the implications of withdrawal versus support teaching (especially in secondary school)
- allocation to subtype
- the implications for the neuropsychological classification in the school setting.

The role of phonology

In earlier chapters, the classifications of Bakker (1990) have been compared to those of Boder (1973). When the subtypes of Bakker and Boder are compared and contrasted, a fundamental difference concerns the role of phonology. This has impact on the relative proportions of subjects within each subtype. For both workers the role of phonology directly affects allocation to subtype.

The first characteristic that distinguishes Bakker's model of reading development from those of other workers is the role of phonological skills. Traditionally within the literature, phonological awareness is thought to be a linguistic (therefore left hemisphere-mediated activity). The Balance Model assumes phonological conversion is linked to right hemisphere processing as a result of the initial visual analysis of single graphemes. Grace and Spreen (1995) question this and also whether it can be argued that phonological coding is a visuo-perceptual measure. The differences of emphasis can be examined. In other developmental models, emphasis on visual analysis is expressed only for whole-word recognition or for the direct route to text access. This is in contrast with the indirect route of phonological decoding using alphabetic principles. Within the Bakker theory both elements find synthesis in a visual-perceptual strategy and there is no clear distinction between holistic (whole word) and analytic (phonemic) processing. In a fine-grained analysis it is difficult to distinguish visual from linguistic strategies. Perceptual analysis affects both whole-

116

word recognition and individual letter recognition in morpheme recognition. Grace and Spreen write of the need to identify the level at which the analysis is performed and the processes that are activated.

Hemispheric involvement in the reading process is complex and this could be apparent in phonological awareness. Certain phonological processes, though involving sounds, also have a visual component, as letter recognition is initially a visual activity. The salient details of the letter form are analysed visually before the next stage of letter naming occurs. At this stage, phoneme assembly, which has a clear auditory/linguistic component, occurs.

It is in this context that the differences between Boder and Bakker are evident. Boder classifies as dysphonetic the child who cannot respond to phonetic analysis and prefers the visual gestalt. The Bakker model classifies this child as the child who has an over-reliance on phonics and is therefore a P-type. Both have a central difficulty with the appropriate use of phonics; one (the dysphonetic) underuses grapheme–phoneme conversion and one (the P-type) uses it excessively and therefore inappropriately. This directly affects the proportion of pupils within the subtype categories. Within the Boder classification the dysphonetic group is the larger, with an estimated 62% belonging to this category. Estimated coverage by the three groups of dysphonetic, dyseidetic and mixed, is 84%.

In contrast, the Bakker classification has coverage at 60% for the two categories of P-type and L-type. If the subtypology is extended to include the M subtype, who demonstrate certain elements from both groups, then coverage is improved. If the Balance Model is viewed developmentally, pupils make the transition from the initial perceptual reading to the linguistic stage when their reading skill is sufficient. Pupils in the mixed category could conceivably be in a transition from one stage to another. They could be assimilating new strategies from the next stage of reading development. This may lead to fluctuations in their observed reading behaviour, while the new skills are gaining mastery.

Within the Bakker model the largest category is the L-type classification (problems in the visual modality), which comprise approximately 32% of the 60% population who could be classified. (The P-type subjects who have problems in the auditory modality are estimated at approximately 28% only.) This is in direct contrast to the Boder figures, wherein the auditory difficulties (dysphonetic) are the largest group. If the role of phonological awareness were consistent between workers and typologies, this difference might not be so apparent. Such differences may highlight the importance of classification, particularly if differential subtype × material interactions are sought. It is therefore crucial that pupils are classified correctly and consistently.

The difficulties of allocating pupils to subtype categories have been discussed in Chapter 3. Currently it is clear that different workers have used different dimensions as the basis of subtype allocation. Some have used reading speed, error analysis and ear advantage, while others have used one or two of these aspects only. It cannot, therefore be judged that an L-type in one study would be an L-type in another study. This is problematic and does mean that the current method of pupil classification is in need of refinement. However, if the findings of Johnson and Robertson (1999) are validated, the factor which impacts on pupil perform-ance is more likely to be the type of materials provided for the pupil than the pupil's original classification. In some ways, if this were confirmed, it would nullify the problems of subtype allocation and would make teaching decisions rest on observed deficits in reading performance. It is interesting that in all the interviews with teachers, they had opinions as to which type of intervention was more in keeping with pupil needs (Robertson 1996).

It is also clear that identification of subtypes within the school setting will be problematic and may be compounded by using samples of pupils statemented as being dyslexic. This may be due to a combination of factors, which include the identification of pupil difficulties in reading accuracy as being a powerful determin-ant in identification. The implications of this will be considered in respect of current practices within both primary and secondary schools.

Implications for the L- and P-type pupils within the school system

A central premise of this book has been that the Bakker subtypes exist and will be found within a certain proportion in all schools. The nature of their reading diffi-culties will determine how easily and at what stage of their school career they are identified. The possibility of recognition of pupils within the relative subtypes may, in part, depend on the subtype to which they belong. It could vary for pupils in either category depending on differences in identification or assessment processes or the way the reading task is viewed within the school system.

It is interesting that from a statemented sample in the UK there are generally more pupils subsequently identified as L-types, yet within samples of pupils who are not statemented, the proportion of P-types increases. In a study conducted as part of her PhD research, Filippatou (personal communication, 1996) found four P-type pupils in a random sample of ten primary school pupils. None of the pupils was statemented, but the teacher had nominated them as being in need of additional support with their reading. This could be an area to merit further inves-tigation, as the implications may reflect the differences in identification which have been documented previously. The implications and outcomes could also be different within the primary and the secondary school.

L- and P-type dyslexia in the primary school

Within primary schools there is, quite rightly, an emphasis on literacy acquisition. This has recently gained momentum with the advent of the National Literacy

Strategy (DfEE 1998a). The reading progress of pupils is monitored and the acquisition of literacy is considered a legitimate priority within the curriculum. Reading is considered a subject area in its own right. This may occasion improvements in reading standards but, to date, there have existed certain pupils who experience reading failure from the outset. Text remains unfathomable and the children become increasingly puzzled as to how other children can access text so easily. Some are severely affected by repeated failure and suffer reduced self-esteem. They may lose all interest in the reading process and perceive it as irrelevant to them. If the children are fortunate, the extent of their difficulties may be recognized and they may be given access to skilled and appropriate support. The access to early intervention allows for damage to self-esteem to be repaired. Unfortunately, this is not the scenario for all children and may be partly dependent on the subtype to which the child belongs. The educational implications of two of the case studies previously reported may illustrate this point.

Case study 1: Paul

Paul is 10 years old. The primary school he attends recently became concerned about the level of his reading. As a result of assessment in basic subjects prior to transfer to secondary school, the school realized that his reading age was in excess of two and a half years below his chronological age. They realized there would be some decrement for this boy, but were surprised to discover the extent of it. His class teacher was surprised, as she had never found the pupil to display any aversion to reading. He read slowly but could attempt unknown words using sound/symbol correspondence. His knowledge of letter sounds was good and had shown great improvement since his parents had obtained a private tutor for him at the age of $9\frac{1}{2}$ years. At that time his reading had been causing concern but he had made good progress as a result of the intervention of his tutor. This had been demonstrated by his reading test result at the end of that school year. In a standardized test of reading he had gained one year from his previous results. (The test administered was an untimed reading test of single words. Scoring was for accuracy of decoding only. Neither reading rate nor reading comprehension were assessed by this particular measure.)

When a qualitative assessment of his reading was carried out (NARA) the true extent of his difficulties became apparent. He took two minutes to read a passage of 35 words. The word 'had' appeared on three occasions: each time he decoded it letter-by-letter. Of the four comprehension questions posed, he answered only one correctly and that was at a very low level of literal comprehension. (Picture clues only would have sufficed to deduce this accurately.) It was interesting that all but two of his reading errors were of the fragmentation type. Under the conditions of the Neale Analysis, these were not classified as errors according to the standardized scoring for this particular test, as they were hesitations or letter-by-letter decoding, which resulted ultimately in the right word. The extent of impairment of his access to text was made apparent by his low comprehension score, but must have been a common feature of the reading task for this obviously P-type pupil.

Due to the initial reading measurement instrument selected, the full extent of this pupil's difficulties was concealed. His apparently good word-attack strategies led to his reading ability being overestimated. Comprehension difficulties were not detected. Rate of reading was not considered problematic, as rate of reading is rarely assessed by teachers, but there is evidence that if attention is directed to explicit decoding only, comprehension is affected.

Fortunately for this boy, the extent of his difficulties was correctly identified in primary school. If it had remained undetected until secondary school the increased demands of the text would have caused even greater difficulties for him. It is perhaps a legitimate concern that pupils of this type may go undetected within the school system. Though speculative, this could be one reason why pupils of this subtype, who are statemented as having specific learning difficulties, are rare within the school population. The danger for these pupils is that their superficial decoding skills may mask the full extent of their difficulties with text access and therefore deprive them of early intervention.

Case study 2: Karen

Karen is 8 years old. Her reading was causing extreme concern at the primary school to which she had recently transferred. Her teacher was concerned that she was making no progress with her reading, despite being given some individual support by a specialist teacher within the school. The core vocabulary in the school reading scheme was not being retained consistently, even though she had supportive parents and was taking a reading book home every night. The teachers were puzzled, in that the girl seemed articulate and had superficially good command of spoken language. Her reading performance was clearly causing concern. She made good use of picture clues and could often retell the story, but made many errors with even simple text and appeared sometimes to make wild guesses at unknown words. There was no evidence of any word-attack strategies. Words were either known or unknown. On standardized assessments of reading accuracy the girl did not score. As a consequence of this, comprehension could not be assessed, but superficially the pupil appeared to derive some meaning from the text. This pupil was very quickly identified by the teacher as having a severe reading difficulty. One could even speculate that this could have been detected earlier had this pupil not had two changes of primary school.

Detection of difficulties for this pupil was obviously quicker than for Paul, and access to specialist intervention was provided earlier. The nature and extent of the difficulties were easy to detect. There were no skills to mask the extent of the difficulties with reading.

Of these two cases it would be impossible to say who had the greater need. Reading for both had failed, if the intention of reading is to communicate. Yet one subtype will often be identified earlier than the other because of the nature of their difficulties and the way in which reading is assessed within the primary school. For one pupil, it was the chance use of a different measure which led to the qualitative assessment that revealed his difficulties. For the other, the difficulties were all too apparent and led to early (and successful) intervention.

L- and P-type dyslexia in the secondary school

In secondary school, it is often assumed that the basics of literacy are in place and that reading, as a subject in its own right, should no longer be pursued. By this time, reading is viewed as a medium for learning new subject areas. It thus becomes a means of access to further learning.

The secondary school curriculum is delivered largely by printed texts. These may be referred to within classes and are often followed up as homework tasks. The specialized nature of the curriculum means it will be delivered by subject teachers and there may be many changes of teacher within the school day. On the teachers' part, they may have contact with in excess of 100 pupils per week, therefore knowledge of individual pupils is problematic. The nature and extent of pupil difficulties may be undetected, yet the way the curriculum is delivered may make increased demands on the pupils' literacy skills. Fortunate pupils may have access to specialist support, but even with support there may be a consistent mismatch between the independent reading level of pupils and the text, which may be at frustration level for these pupils. There is thus an urgent need to broaden the range of strategies available to both class and specialist teachers in order for pupil literacy to be improved.

For the class teacher the onus may be on increased ability to identify pupils whose literacy difficulties are not progressing on the varied measures of accuracy, comprehension and rate of reading. The implications for consistent performance on all of these need to be considered. For the specialist teacher, the challenge may be to increase the repertoire of their skills so that strategies such as neuropsychological methods of intervention can be utilized in the short term to facilitate text access in the long term.

All studies of neuropsychological intervention have clearly prescribed time limits. It is certainly not intended to provide a long-term perspective; rather to allow pupil response to text to be adapted over a period of weeks. The optimum period for intervention would seem to be about 16 weeks and the latest research from the Netherlands is advocating an additional two sessions after intervention has ceased. During this time it will, in most cases, become increasingly evident whether or not the intervention is changing the superficial response to text. Most teachers who have used the approach have confirmed that the different reading style was transferred to other more general reading tasks and showed clearly as either a more accurate response to text or a more fluent response to text.

Other teachers have commented on the increased spelling ability. The author has not studied impact on spelling in all cases but can confirm that the pupils who used the hemisphere-specific approach superficially improved in their ability to use the alphabetic code in their spelling. This may be seen as contributing to spelling development, certainly in the first instance. This is clearly another area that requires further study, as spelling difficulties may be both more severe and more entrenched for the pupil with dyslexia. It is also noteworthy that this approach has not been documented as being used with adult subjects. This again may be an area to benefit from further study so that the range of strategies of those supporting adult students can be increased. In this case the materials would need careful selection so as not to appear patronizing and inappropriate to the students. All of these elements merit study both in controlled experimental and field conditions to help improve the current provision available for dyslexic people.

Validity of the L- and P-type classification within the school

When teachers learn of the Balance Model and the L and P classification, the number who comment that it confirms what they observe in the classroom is striking. Teachers are expert at observing and catering for individual differences. They see differences in their pupils' rate of learning and they have considerable expertise in detecting when learning is not progressing at the normal rate. Improvements in initial teacher education now mean that all teachers are given some input on meeting the needs of children with special educational needs. Increased expertise is now a central feature in the standards for teachers. This will improve the expectation of success for pupils in the schools. There is also increased knowledge within the teaching profession on the teaching of reading, and such government initiatives as the National Literacy Strategy can be considered an important step in the right direction. Thus teachers are more conversant with the nature of the reading task and its varied task demands.

Increasingly in initial teacher education, some input on dyslexia is delivered as a core element and is welcomed by students, who recognize the importance of this issue in enabling them subsequently to discharge their professional responsibilities with maximum effect (DfEE 1998b). This must be an important step in raising the level of teacher awareness of individual needs. If mainstream teachers improve their ability to identify and refer children before they have experienced entrenched failure in the reading task, this will have an important preventive function. If teachers are more knowledgeable they may become more able to appreciate the complexity of the pattern of difficulties presented by the child with specific learning difficulties. Their difficulties present a greater challenge, and once they are detected usually require specialist approaches for the child to make optimum progress.

Within the framework of specialist provision, the L- and P-type classification can provide an alternative method of considering pupils. Targeted intervention directed at the pupil's neuropsychologically based needs can then be devised and implemented. At present, it cannot be said that this will benefit all children, but extension of the work may lead to a greater facility in identifying those pupils for whom the approach is of value. In the event, this could extend the knowledge base of both the similarities and the differences between pupils and further extend the theoretical study of the aetiology of dyslexia into the essential realm of intervention.

With regard to intervention, there are some questions to be answered. If the majority of pupils who have specific learning difficulties have been identified on the basis of decrements in reading accuracy, then the L-type materials will be more effective in compensating for the observed deficits in information processing of text. Once reading accuracy has been improved, there will be a need for the reading process to begin to concentrate on the fluent reading of the accomplished reader, where clues are derived from the semantic or meaning aspects of the text. This may justify the developmental model for intervention, wherein one hemisphere is stimulated initially, followed by stimulation of the opposing hemisphere. This may be seen to have taken into consideration the identified needs of the reading process with regard to the individual pupil. Although, to the author's knowledge, there are no recorded studies of neuropsychological intervention being undertaken with adults, this would also be a useful direction to pursue. A similar extension of this work could include studies involving children with more general reading difficulties.

The focus of this book has been identified as students with dyslexia, and the reported studies from the UK have been based on students who are identified as having specific learning difficulties. Yet certain of the studies from the Netherlands do not involve such a specific sample. It can be speculated that, if neuropsychological intervention is based on a developmental model of the reading process (the Balance Model), the intervention should also hold promise for any reader who is experiencing difficulty in gaining skill in the varied aspects of reading accuracy or reading fluency. This again is intended to be the focus of further study and is an element in which both specialist and mainstream teachers express interest.

Conclusions

A central conclusion of this work would seem to be that neuropsychological intervention can be a useful addition to the range of strategies available to teachers who are responsible for improving the reading ability of dyslexic pupils. The strengths are that the approach can be tailored to either identified pupil subtype or the observed needs of pupils, in relation to the information processing abilities necessary for successful reading. A central advantage is that the duration of the intervention will be limited to a maximum of approximately 20 weeks, in sharp contrast to the long-term intervention currently being used and, if beneficial, could usefully become one part of such long-term provision.

Two other very positive findings from many studies in neuropsychological intervention concern the transfer of skill from the neuropsychological materials to other textual materials and the duration of impact after intervention has ceased. These factors are persistent problems and are frequently reported by teachers of pupils with dyslexia. Both can be equally frustrating for teachers and pupils alike, who have jointly struggled for a particular aspect to be learned, only to find that the skill is either not utilized within the classroom context or is not retained after even a short break from teaching. This approach could therefore be useful in helping to overcome these recorded difficulties. The impact not only on reading but also on spelling ability would seem to hold promise for further study, particularly if neuropsychological intervention is confirmed as being effective in allowing grapheme–phoneme correspondence to be attained. Essentially, the method has been found to be successful in enabling some dyslexic pupils to overcome their reading difficulties. The impact on spelling also requires systematic investigation.

It would be too simplistic to infer that the approach could in any way 'cure' dyslexia with its complex patterns of cognitive difficulties. It may, however, be seen as a method that offers some promise in facilitating the development of the effective reading and spelling skills, which can increase educational success for certain dyslexic pupils.

Appendix 1
Classification method

Substantive errors

1   **Substitutions erroneously read words** (resulting in a non-existent word)

la   Letter, number of letters or syllables not read, e.g. table...tab

lb   Letter, number of letters or syllables wrongly added to the word, e.g. run...runned

lc   Letter, number of letters or syllables read wrongly, e.g. skinny...skippy

2   **Erroneously read words** (resulting in an existing word)

2a   Synonym (word same meaning), e.g. The dog is (small) little

2b   Semantically acceptable word (not a synonym), e.g. The dog is big

2c   Not a semantically acceptable word (also not a synonym), e.g. The dog is cat

3   **Omissions (of both words and sentences)**

3a   Word omitted, e.g. Mum is (in) the house

3b   Sentence or part of a sentence omitted

3c   Whole line of text omitted

4   **Additions**

4a   Single word added to the text, e.g. She has a (big) dog

5   **Reversals**

5a   Letters or syllables reversed (within a word), e.g. bad...dab

5b   Sequence of words reversed (within a sentence), e.g. She jumps and runs

6   **Pronunciations**

6a   Words pronounced inaccurately

Fragmentation or time-consuming errors

7   **Spelling, stammering-like reading**

7a   Word or part of a word read in spelling-like fashion (not synthesized), e.g. t-r-a-p

7b   Word or part of a word read in spelling-like fashion (synthesized), e.g. t-r-a-p...trap

8   **Repetitions***
8a   Word repeated one or more times
8b   Part of sentence (more than one word) repeated one or more times
8c   Whole sentence repeated one or more times

*Not to be scored if the child is correcting a previous error. Corrected error only to be scored

9   **Corrections***
9a   A substantive error is corrected

*In the case of a correction, the child scores two errors: one substantive (original error) and one fragmentation (correction)

10   **Hesitation**
10a Child hesitates (stipulate time beforehand for consistency)

Scoring procedure

It is suggested that the reading be taped, so that detailed subsequent analysis can take place. From the taped analysis, the number of errors in each category should be itemized and counted. A group mean (average) for each type of error should be calculated. The 'L-type' pupil makes more than the average number of substantive errors and fewer than average fragmentation errors. The 'P-type' pupil shows the reverse profile, having more fragmentation errors. Some pupils make almost equivalent number of both types of errors, therefore they can be termed 'M-type' pupils. If the teacher is using this approach on an individual as opposed to a group, the number of errors of each type made by the pupil is easily counted. This can be supplemented with prior knowledge of the pupil's general approach to reading. (Detailed guidance of the error analysis process can be found in the classification examples given in Chapter 3.)

Appendix 2
Examples of materials for L-type and P-type pupils

This section contains some examples of the type of materials suitable for each of the respective subtypes. Some of the examples show how the material presented to the pupil can be adapted to allude (or appeal to) one hemisphere over the other. These could be used to supplement traditional approaches and may form the basis of teacher-made resources, with an additional element being hemispheric stimulation.

The appropriate materials in this section may be photocopied and used directly with pupils.

The examples are presented in two sections: the first showing the adaptation for L-type pupils and the second the adaptation for P-type pupils.

Example 1 (L-type materials)

There are two words jumbled up. One word is in capital letters and the other is in lower case (small) letters. Can you find which words they are?

HwOiUlSlE

SbHoOyP

PdLoAgY

SfTrRoEmET

AwBeOnUtT

LuInKdEer

MhAeKrEe

TsHhEeM

DtOhWeN

LhOiOmK

Example 2 (L-type materials)

There are two words jumbled up. One word is in capital letters and the other is in lower case (small) letters. Can you find which words they are?

AoBvOeUrT

MmAaDnE

ObViEgR

BsEeEeN

BrAuCnK

DwOhWoN

BrLeAaCdK

DbOuOtR

WgIrNeDeOnW

WaAnNdT

DfOoWrN

TsHaAwT

Example 3 (L-type materials)

There are two words jumbled up. One word is in capital letters and the other is in lower case (small) letters. Can you find which words they are?

HaEnRdE

FsAhSeT

AbWoAyY

BcRaImNeG

TdHaEyN

EfAaCrH

BeAnBdY

HmEaAnD

LnOoOwK

MsUaCwH

MuAnNdYer

MtUoSoT

Example 4 (L-type materials)

There are two words jumbled up. One word is in capital letters and the other is in lower case (small) letters. Can you find which words they are?

CtLhOaCnK

UtNhDiEsR

TfHoErN

TsHtIaNyG

WyAoNuT

TwIaMsE

WaErEeK

RcEaAnD

TrHuEnM

MdIaLyK

TsAhKeE

BhReIrNeG

Example 5 (L-type materials)

There are two words jumbled up. One word is in capital letters and the other is in lower case (small) letters. Can you find which words they are?

PwLaAyY

OsPaEyN

JaUnMyP

KmEaEyP

LnAeSwT

LhIoTuTsLeE

BnLoUwE

MoUfCfH

OsNhCeE

PwLhAoY

SyAeIsD

TmHaAnT

Example 6 (L-type materials)

The following example was prepared for pupils with a higher reading accuracy age, but who display perceptual carelessness to text.

SpClHaOOyL

BcRaOmTpHiEnRg

FsOOlTiBdAeLL

PhLaAmYbGuRrOgUeNrD

WpIlNaTnEtR

SuOmMbErTeHlIlNaG

ApDoVsEsNiTbUlReE

TrEuLcEkVsIaScIkON

ShOiMsEtToIrMyES

CpOrMoPbUlTeEmR

Example 7 (L-type materials)

The following example was prepared for pupils with a higher reading accuracy age, but who display perceptual carelessness to text.

CeAlNbDoLwE

ChLoApSeSlReOsOsM

AcNaYrWpHeEtRsE

WpHaOpEeVrEsR

ShEiPtTtEMiBnEgR

RtAaIrNgBeOtW

FpLlOaWyEeRd

EwLiBnOeW

BdUrTeTaEmReFrLY

WsHcIrSaTpLeE

Example 8 (L-type materials)

The following example was prepared for pupils with a higher reading accuracy age, but who display perceptual carelessness to text.

ChAoSpTeLdE

KdEiTvTeLrE

SaIcXrToEsEsN

SwEiVnEdNoTwY

GhRoOnUeNyD

GbArRoDwEnN

WbAaTbCyH

BhEaCpApMyE

WsIlToCwH

BeRlOeOpMhSaTnItCsK

Example 9 (L-type materials)

The following example was prepared for pupils with a higher reading accuracy age, but who display perceptual carelessness to text.

ScTlRaAwP

SmNiOdWdDlReOP

LtUiNnCsH

SgHaEpEsT

NlEeEtD

SwWaEtEeTrSs

SoTvAeRrT

QfUlIaCnK

PbLoAtStTlIeCs

TaAbRoGvEeT

Example 10 (L-type materials)

(It should be noted that here, letters which are perceptually similar have been deliberately substituted. Normally these are used with care, but here they have been included deliberately to add to the perceptual challenge for the pupil.)

These sentences look almost the same. Some letters are different, can you find which they are?

Sam ran down the hill fast and fell down in the stream.

Sap ram domn the hill fats and fell bown in the slrean.

The ball hit the window and the glass fell on the dog.

Tha dall het the miudom anb the ghass feii on tne dag.

I went in the shop to get a drink.

L weul im thi stop ta gel a brink.

I have a little dog called Scamp.

I hene o lillte doq catted Skanp.

On Wednesday I go swimming with my school.

Om Webuesbag I ga smiwwinp wihl mg sctoaal.

Example 11 (L-type materials)

These sentences look the same. Which letters are different?

I had a drink of milk and cake at supper time.

I bab a duiuk fo mihk anb oale ah suqqer tiwe.

The sun was very hot on Monday.

Tha snu wos werg nol ou Woubag.

My dad went to work in the new red car.

Mg bab weuh ta mock iu tfe uew rab oar.

I like to ride my bike in the park.

I life ta hiba mq bihe iu fhe pack.

I have a sister called Pam. She is six years old.

I bane a slsfer catteb Paw. Sho ls slx jeors alb.

I saw a good film on TV on Sunday.

I sam a doog fihm an TV un Snubay.

Example 12 (L-type materials)

If you put these letters in order of size, they make a word. Can you find them?

g   **b**   n   a

p   m   **j**   u

a   y   l   **p**

e   **k**   **m**   a

m   t   e   **h**

n   **W**   t   e

Example 13 (L-type materials)

The letters in these words are in the wrong order. Can you find the word?

1. Sdai

2. Rnu

3. Meka

4. Hdie

5. Fndi

6. Hple

7. Hree

8. Fsta

9. Hlil

10. Hsoue

Can you find the words in these rows of letters? What do they say?

1   Pamewjfrwentjdtokfthemgndnhshopmgksfgonjdgsfherndnjbike.

2   I fngndflikedjnfjsndtokfdsmsmfplayfgnjwithnbmymkdssadog.

3   InldgjsummerjngjImdskkgplaymjngjfinjnjngjthejdnjspark.

4   Iwernwejhjhwentndsjjtomtheasjashopkwhenjfdjnmumkdwasphuill.

5   Imnjnlikemdsnfsjmykdsjnewmndfjnsreadingkdsjfsbook.

Example 14 (L-type materials)

Here are some words and shapes. Can you find the ones that have both the same shape and the same word?

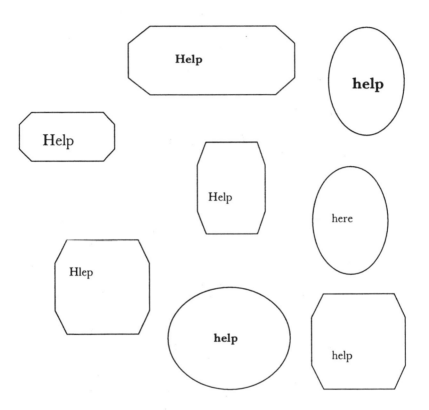

Example 15 (L-type materials)

Here are some more words and shapes. Can you match the words and shapes that are the same?

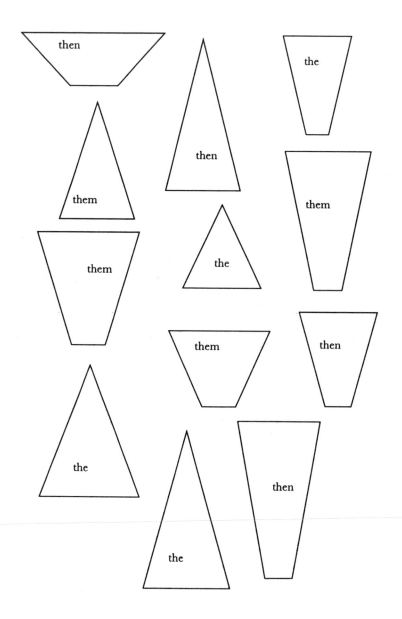

Example 1 (P-type materials)

The following exercise is for P-type pupils and is designed to encourage semantic interaction with the text.

There is one word too many in these sentences. Which one is it?

Sam went to the bus red stop.

I can run very big fast.

Mum took me to the duck park.

My school bag went is black.

My Dad has a park new black car.

I went to the park with like Mike.

The door of my house are is red.

I had fish and apple chips for tea.

I went on the bus to hand school.

The ends of these sentences are mixed up. Can you sort them out?

I like to	park the to go.
I got an apple	the at shops.
My bike can	very go fast.
Dad got me	new football a.
When I ran down the hill	fell over I.
My dog likes to play	ball a with.

Example 2 (P-type materials)

The following exercise is for P-type pupils and is designed to encourage semantic interaction with the text.

There is one word too many in these sentences. Can you find which one it is?

1. The cat likes to drink red milk.

2. Mum took me to the table shop.

3. I like to play with my over sister.

4. Dad went to black work this morning.

5. Mum made me a new winter tree coat.

6. I fell over and broke my new chin watch.

7. The cat jumped up the put tree.

8. My dog likes to run after in cats.

The ends of these sentences are mixed up. Can you sort them out?

1. Last week I   seaside the to went.

2. The name of   cat my little Fluff is.

3. The bus stop is   gate park the at.

4. The red car went   down the road fast very

5. My sister got   new a bike.

6. John can kick   ball the hard very.

Example 3 (P-type materials)

The following exercise is for P-type pupils and is designed to encourage semantic interaction with the text.

These sentences have one word too many. Can you work out which one it is?

1. I like to read my rug book after tea.

2. My best friend is tape Linda.

3. The car did not out stop in time.

4. I can go to the bag market after tea.

5. The ball went in the window with a crash red.

6. I had a blue bump in my new car.

7. The dog bit me on the book leg.

8. Dad got me a new yellow pen over for school.

The ends of these sentences are mixed up. Can you sort them out?

1. In the holidays   I park the to went.

2. The cat ran away   dog from the.

3. The water in the   hot bath was.

4. I went for a   bike my on ride.

5. The cup of tea   milk no in it had.

6. The red apples   tree the on were.

Example 4 (P-type materials)

The following exercise is for P-type pupils and is designed to encourage semantic interaction with the text.

There is one word too many in these sentences. Can you work out which one it is?

1. My cat likes to play up with string.

2. Mum took me to play on the table swings.

3. My sister was ill last but week.

4. Can I put the black chair back hand now?

5. My Dad goes to work on the stop bus.

6. Today I went for a blue swim.

7. The duck swam on the plant pond.

8. John had a hat for the sea winter.

The ends of these sentences are mixed up. Can you sort them out?

1. The duck can   pond the swim on.

2. The tea cup   broke and down fell.

3. I went on the   park slide the in.

4. The stick   pond the in fell.

5. The bird made   nest my garden a in.

6. The little bird   nest the in sat.

7. Tom ran back   hill the up.

Example 5 (P-type materials)

The following exercise is for P-type pupils and is designed to encourage semantic interaction with the text.

These words are not in the right order for the alphabet. Can you put them in the right order?

1. road

2. school

3. car

4. wednesday

5. mother

6. dog

7. here

8. bring

9. jump

10. no

11. pet

12. take

How many words can you make from these sets of letters?

a p t s a n I l c   l k I r a p g e

t s a f m u d r I   h p e l a m r f

Example 6 (P-type materials)

The following exercise is for P-type pupils and is designed to encourage semantic interaction with the text.

Can you find words that rhyme with those in the first box?

Cap	l-	m-
Sat	m-	p-
Hid	d-	l-
Top	m-	st-
Dan	m-	r-
Fill	m-	h-
Lit	h-	p-
Red	b-	f-

Example 7 (P-type materials)

The following exercise is for P-type pupils and is designed to encourage semantic interaction with the text.

Which of these words rhyme?

Cat	Sit	mat
Pen	Hand	den
Run	Man	can
Hill	Bell	fell
Cup	Map	sap
Lad	Hid	sad
Rip	Slip	nap
Red	Head	had
And	Land	send

These sentences are in the wrong order. Can you sort them out?

My sister to school back went to.

Dog my fast run can.

Ship sea the I on saw a.

Week next I football am to going.

Night last party I had a garden the in.

I happy playing park the in am.

Example 8 (P-type materials)

The following exercise is for P-type pupils and is designed to encourage semantic interaction with the text.

Here is a story but the order of the sentences is wrong. Can you make it right?

1. Then they went home.

2. Tim had a birthday.

3. He got up and had some toast.

4. They played lots of games.

5. At tea-time they had a party.

6. He got lots of cards in the post.

7. All his friends from school came.

8. He woke up at seven.

9. He looked out of the window and saw the sun shining.

10. His Uncle Ben came to help.

One of the words in the list does not fit in. Which one ?

1.	aunt	uncle		farmer	
2.	book		paper		hand
3.	fat		thin		hot
4.	arm	leg		hat	
5.	sun		rain		help

Example 9 (P-type materials)

The following exercise is for P-type pupils and is designed to encourage semantic interaction with the text.

The sentences in these passages are mixed up. Can you make them into four short stories?

Kelly ran into the house and heard the phone ring.

She ran home from school fast.

When she picked it up it was her friend Ben.

She was very happy when she was on the beach.

When she woke up the sun was shining.

Mum said it was a good day for a picnic.

They got into the car and set off.

Sam was good and saved a lot of goals.

They played in the big park at the top of the hill.

Sam was happy when he was playing football.

Sam liked it best when he was in goal.

The dog ran away as it was scared.

The big red car was going too fast.

A little brown dog was crossing the road.

Example 10 (P-type materials)

The following exercise is for P-type pupils and is designed to encourage semantic interaction with the text.

There are words are missing from these sentences. Do you know what they are?

1. I ran very to get the bus.

2. In the winter I like to a snowman.

3. I went to the to get some milk.

4. My sister down and cut her leg.

5. I a new bike for my birthday.

6. On Monday I went to and we had football.

7. I saw the in the field.

8. The train under the railway bridge.

9. The of my dog is Gruff.

10. The sheepdog ran the sheep in the field.

What is wrong with these sentences?

1. In winter I like to lie in the sunshine.

2. The man bit the dog on the leg.

3. The fox got on the bus in the town.

4. The jelly ran into the bank.

5. All my friends like to eat twigs.

Glossary of terms

Alphabetic. Second stage of the Frith model of reading and spelling, where there are the beginnings of knowledge of letters and letter-sounds.

Angular gyrus. This is a gyrus (or ridge) in the parietal lobe, which is important in language function.

Anterior (front). This is an indicator of anatomical direction in relation to other structures on the cortex.

Aphasia. A defect or loss of power of expression by speech, writing or signs, or of comprehending spoken or written language due to injury or disease of the brain.

Arcuate fasciculus. A long bundle of fibres linking Broca's area of language production to Wernicke's area for language comprehension.

Asymmetry. The normal pattern of cerebral asymmetry is that the left hemisphere is usually larger than the right hemisphere.

Bilateral. Cortical structures are on both sides of the cortex.

Broca's area. Region of the left frontal lobe thought to be involved in the production of language. Resultant damage being termed 'Broca's aphasia'.

Cerebellum. The cerebellum is a major structure of the hind brain and is specialized in motor co-ordination.

Cingulate cortex. A strip of limbic cortex lying just above the corpus callosum along the medial wall of the cerebral hemispheres.

Computerized tomography or CT scan. The use of a complex software program converts the MRI image into a 3D image of the part of the body under investigation. The result is an 'X-ray picture' of the soft tissue.

Conduction or conduct aphasia. A type of fluent aphasia in which despite alleged normal comprehension of spoken language, words are repeated incorrectly due to an inability to translate heard, written or self-generated words into phonemic or sound sequences.

Contralateral. This is where cortical structures are on opposite sides of the cortex.

Corpus callosum. A fibre system connecting the two hemispheres of the brain.

153

Cortex. Latin word for the bark of a tree. Used interchangeably with neocortex. It comprises most of the forebrain and consists of four to six layers (grey matter).

Cytoarchitectonic research. This is research concerning the organization, structure and distribution of cells.

Dendrites. These are extensions of the cell body that increase the surface area and are specialized to receive information from other cells.

Dysphonetic. This is a Boder subtype category showing an inability to access a phonological route to words. There is a reliance on visual or whole-word strategies.

Dyseidetic. This is a Boder subtype category showing an inability to access words by a whole-word or visual approach. There is reliance on a phonological strategy.

Electrophysiological studies (either electroencephalogram, EEG, or event-related potential, ERP). These both measure brain activity by placing electrodes at strategic points on the skull. The ERP technique presents a stimulus (either visual or auditory) to the subject undergoing the EEG and measures the type of activity generated.

Electroencephalogram (EEG). Technique that measures brain activity by placing electrodes at specific points on the skull.

Event-related potential (ERP). This measures brain activity by placing electrodes at strategic points on the skull. The ERP technique presents a stimulus (either visual or auditory) to the subject undergoing the EEG and measures the type of activity generated.

Fissure. A deep cleft on the cortex.

Functional MRI (fMRI). This extends the basic picture from the MRI by revealing the areas of greatest brain activity. Glucose and oxygen, both of which are carried in the blood, fuel neuronal firing. When an area of the brain is activated, these substances flow towards it and the fMRI can demonstrate the areas that have most oxygen, depending on the amount of activity. Modern scans are now capable of producing images every four seconds so that any changes in activity according to the task demands are revealed.

Graphemes. These are groups of letters that can be understood without being sounded out, they are the written representation of words.

Grey matter. This is any brain area composed mainly of cell bodies.

Gyrus. A ridge on the cortex (plural gyri).

Ipsilateral. This means cortical structures are on the same side of the cortex and not on opposing hemispheres.

Lateral (side). An indicator of anatomical direction in relation to other structures on the cortex.

Lateral geniculate nucleus. Part of the thalamus and involved in vision.

Lexicon. Dictionary or memory store in the brain that contains memory of words and their meanings.

Logographic. First stage of the Frith model of reading and spelling development. At this stage response is to whole picture of a word.

Magnetic resonance imaging (MRI). The MRI technique aligns atomic particles in the tissue by magnetism and then bombards them with radio waves. The bombarded particles emit radio signals, which differ according to the type of tissue present.

Medial (middle). An indicator of anatomical direction in relation to other structures on the cortex.

Morphemes. These are the smallest units of language which carry meaning and could include suffixes and prefixes.

Myelination. This is the process by which the support cells of the nervous system surround and insulate axons and is sometimes used as an index of maturation.

Neocortex. Latin word for the bark of a tree. Used interchangeably with cortex. It comprises most of the forebrain and consists of four to six layers (grey matter).

Occipital lobe. General area of the cortex located in the back part of the head and important in the visual process.

Optic chiasma. This is a crossing point for the optic nerves and is central to the process of visual perception.

Orthographic stage. Final stage according to the Frith model. At this point there is less reliance on sound-symbol correspondence than on conventions for reading and spelling.

Orthography. This is a standardized system for writing a particular language, for example in English we have letter clusters such as 'spl' but not 'wgf'.

Phoneme. Unit of sound that forms a word or part of a word.

Phonological dyslexia. This is a form of dyslexia in which words cannot be accessed by grapheme–phoneme (letter–sound) correspondence. There is also inability to read non-words aloud.

Phrenology. A long discredited study of the relationship between mental faculties and the surface features of the skull.

Plasticity. This is the ability of the brain to change in various ways to compensate for loss of function due to damage.

Positron emission topography (PET). These scans are successful in identifying the brain areas that are most involved in a given task by measuring the amount of fuel consumed.

Posterior (back). Indicator of anatomical direction in relation to other structures on the cortex.

Prosody. The variation in stress, pitch and rhythm of language which convey meaning.

Reversed asymmetry. When the right cerebral hemisphere is larger than the left, as opposed to the more usual pattern of the left hemisphere being larger.

Semantic substitutions. Substituting one word for another with the same meaning, for example substituting the word 'gnome' for 'pixie'.

Somatosensory system. Neural system involving the tactile senses of touch, pain and body awareness.

Split brain research. This is where the two hemispheres of the brain are artificially separated by severing the corpus callosum.

Striate cortex. This is considered to be the primary visual cortex and is the site where visual impressions are relayed.

Sylvian or lateral fissure. This is a deep cleft on the surface of the brain which extends laterally, posteriorly and upwards separating the temporal and parietal lobes.

Synapses. These are the points of contact between the cells.

Sulcus. A shallow cleft on the cortex (plural sulci).

Superior (top). Indicator of anatomical direction in relation to other structures on the cortex.

Ventral (bottom). Indicator of anatomical direction in relation to other structures on the cortex.

Wernicke's area. Posterior portion of the superior temporal gyrus involved in language comprehension.

Word retrieval or naming difficulties. Inability to bring a required word to mind so that a word may be described by function instead of name. Thus a person with naming difficulties might ask 'Could I have that thing to write with please?' instead of 'Could I have that pen?'.

References

Arnold H (1982) Making sense of it: graded passages for miscue analysis. Sevenoaks: Hodder and Stoughton.

Augur J, Briggs S (1994) The Hickey multisensory language course, 2nd edn London: Whurr.

Bakker DJ (1990) Neuropsychological treatment of dyslexia. New York: Oxford University Press.

Bakker DJ (1994) Dyslexia and the ecological brain. Journal of Clinical and Experimental Neuropsychology 16, 734–43.

Bakker DJ (1997) Dyslexia in terms of space and time. 4th World Congress on Dyslexia, Halkidiki, Greece.

Bakker DJ, Bouma A, Gardien CJ (1990) Hemisphere specific treatment of dyslexic sub-types. A field experiment. Learning Disabilities 23, 433-8.

Bakker DJ, Licht R (1986) Learning to read: changing horses in midstream. In Dyslexia: its neuropsychology and treatment (eds GTh Pavlidis, DF Fisher), (pp 87-95). New York: Wiley.

Bakker DJ, Licht R, Kappers EJ (1995) Hemispheric stimulation techniques in children with dyslexia. In Advances in child neuropsychology, vol. 3 (eds MG Tramontana, SR Hooper), (pp 144-77). New York: Springer Verlag.

Bakker DJ, Moerland R, Goekoop-Hoefkens M (1981) Effects of hemisphere-specific stimulation on the reading performance of dyslexic boys: a pilot study. Journal of Clinical Neuropsychology 3, 155-9.

Bakker DJ, Vinke J (1985) Effects of hemisphere-specific stimulation on brain activity and reading. Dyslexics Journal of Clinical and Experimental Neuropsychology 7, 505-25.

Bakker MG, Vonk MI (1998) Hemstim for Windows. The Hague, The Netherlands: Spin Software.

Bateman B (1968) Interpretation of the 1961 Illinois Test of Psycholinguistic Abilities. Seattle: Special Children Publications.

Beard R (1987) Developing reading 3-13. London: Hodder and Stoughton.

Bentin S (1981) On the representation of a second language in the cerebral hemispheres of right-handed people. Neuropsychologia 19, 599-603.

Birch HG, Belmont L (1964) Auditory-visual integration in normal and retarded readers. American Journal Orthopsychiatry 34, 852-61.

Bjargen I, Undheim JO, Nordvik KA, Romslo I (1987) Dyslexia and hormone deficiencies. European Journal of Psychology of Education II, 283-95.

Boden C, Brodeur DA (1999) Visual processing of verbal and nonverbal stimuli in adolescents with reading disabilities. Journal of Learning Disabilities 32, 58-71.

Boder E (1973) Developmental dyslexia: a diagnostic approach based on three atypical reading patterns. Developmental Medicine and Child Neurology 25, 663-87.

Boder E, Jarrico S (1982) The Boder Test of Reading-Spelling Patterns. The Psychological Corporation. London: Harcourt Brace Jovanovich.

Borsting E, Ridder WH 3rd, Dudeck J, Kelley C, Matsui L, Motoyama J (1996) The presence of a magnocellular deficit depends on the type of dyslexia. Vision Research 36, 1047-53.

Bradshaw JL, Gates EA (1978) Visual field differences in verbal tasks: effects of task familiarity and sex of subject. Brain and Language 5, 166-87.

Bradshaw JL, Hicks RE (1977) Word recognition, lexical decision and visual field. Bulletin of the Psychonomic Society 10, 266.

Bruck M (1992) Persistence of dyslexics' phonological awareness deficits. Developmental Psychology 28, 874-86.

Bryant PE, Bradley L, McLean M, Crosland J (1989) Nursery rhymes, phonological skills and reading. Journal of Child Language 16, 407-28.

Bryant PE, Goswami U (1990) Comparisons between backward and normal readers: a risky business. Journal of the Education Section of the British Psychological Society 14, 3–10.

Carter R (1998) Mapping the mind. London: Weidenfeld and Nicolson.

Cornelissen P, Hansen PC, Stein JF (1997) How does magnocellular visual impairment affect reading? 4th World Congress on Dyslexia, Halkidiki, Greece.

Cornelissen P, Richardson A, Mason A, Fowler S, Stein JF (1995) Contrast sensitivity and coherent motion detection measured at phototopic luminance levels in dyslexics and controls. Vision Research 35, 1483-94.

Coslett HB (1991) Read but not write 'idea': evidence for preserved reading in 'pure alexia'. Brain 113, 327-9.

Coslett HB, Monsul N (1994) Reading with the right hemisphere: evidence from transcranial magnetic stimulation. Brain and Language 46, 198-211.

Dalby MA, Elbro C, Stokilde-Jogensen H (1998) Temporal lobe asymmetry and dyslexia. Brain and Language 62, 51-69.

Daniele A, Giustolisi L, Caterina Silver M, Colosimo C, Gainotti G (1994) Evidence for a possible neuroanatomical basis for lexical processing of nouns and verbs. Neuropsychologia 32, 1325-41.

Demb JB, Boynton GM, Best M, Heeger DJ (1998) Psychophysical evidence for a magnocellular pathway deficit in dyslexia. Vision Research 38, 1555-9.

Department of Education and Science (DES) (1994). The Code of Practice on the identification and assessment of special educational needs. London: HMSO.

Department for Education and Employment (DfEE) (1998a) The National Literacy Strategy. London: HMSO.

Department for Education and Employment (DfEE) (1998b) Circular 4/98. Teaching: high status, high standards. Requirements for courses of initial teacher training. London: HMSO.

Dryer R, Beale IV, Lambert AJ (1999) The Balance Model of Dyslexia and Remedial Training: an evaluative study. Journal of Learning Disabilities 32, 174-86.

Eden GF, Stein JF, Wood HM, Wood FB (1996) Differences in visuospatial judgement in reading-disabled and normal children. Perceptual and Motor Skills 82, 155-77.

Edwards VT, Hogben JH, Clark CD, Pratt C (1994) Effects of a red background on magnocellular functioning in average and specifically disabled readers. Vision Research 36, 1037-45.

Eisenberg L (1995) The social construction of the human brain. American Journal of Psychiatry 152, 1563-75.

Fawcett AJ, Nicholson RI (1994) (see page 32).

Fawcett AJ, Nicholson RI (1995) The Dyslexia Early Screening Test (DEST). London: The Psychological Corporation.

Fawcett AJ, Nicholson RI (1996) The Dyslexia Screening Test (DST). London: The Psychological Corporation.

Fawcett AJ, Nicholson RI (1998a) The Dyslexia Adult Screening Test (DAST). London: The Psychological Corporation.

Fawcett AJ, Nicholson RI (1998b) Learning disabilities in adults: screening and diagnosis in the UK. In Bridging the Gap: Learning disabilities, literacy and adult education (eds S Vogel and S Reder). Baltimore: Paul H Brookes.

Fawcett AJ, Nicholson RI, Dean P (1996) Impaired performance of children with dyslexia on a range of cerebellar tasks. Annals of Dyslexia 46, 259-83.

Flynn J, Deering W (1989) Sub-types of dyslexia: investigation of Boder's system using quantitative neurophysiology. Developmental Medicine and Child Neurology 31, 215-23.

Flynn JM, Deering W, Goldstein M, Rahbar MH (1992) Electrophysiological correlates of dyslexic sub-types. Journal of Learning Disabilities 25, 133-41.

Fries CC (1963) Linguistics and reading. New York: Holt, Rinehart & Winston.

Frith U (1985) Beneath the surface in developmental dyslexia. In Surface dyslexia (eds KE Patterson, JC Marshall, M Coltheart). London: Routledge & Kegan Paul.

Frith U (1997) Brain, mind and behaviour in dyslexia. In Dyslexia: Biology, cognition and intervention (eds C Hulme, MJ Snowling). London: Whurr.

Galaburda AM (1989) Ordinary and extraordinary brain development: anatomical variation in developmental Dyslexia. Annals of Dyslexia 39, 67-79.

Galaburda AM, Livingstone M (1993) Evidence for a magnocellular defect in developmental dyslexia. In Temporal information processing in the nervous system (eds P Talla, AM Galaburda, RR Llinas, C von Euler), pp 70-82. New York: The New York Academy of Sciences.

Galloway LM (1982) Bilingualism: neuropsychological considerations. Journal of Research and Development in Education 15, 12-28.

Geschwind N (1965) Disconnection syndromes in animals and man. Parts I and II (Review). Brain 237-94, 585-644.

Geschwind N (1974) The development of the brain and the evolution of language. In Selected Papers on Language and the Brain (ed N Geschwind). Dordrecht, The Netherlands: D Riedel Publishing Co.

Geschwind N (1984) Cerebral dominance in biological perspective. Neuropsychologia 22, 675-83.

Gjessing HJ, Karlsen B (1989) A longitudinal study of dyslexia. New York: Springer-Verlag.

Goldberg E, Costa LD (1981) Hemisphere differences in the acquisition and use of descriptive systems. Brain and Language 14, 144-73.

Goodman KS (1973) Miscues: windows on the reading process. In Miscue analysis: applications to reading instruction ERIC (ed KS Goodman). London: Routledge and Kegan Paul.

Gough PB, Tunmer WE (1986) Decoding, reading and reading disability. Remedial and Special Education 7, 6-10.

Grace GM (1990) Effects of hemisphere-specific stimulation on academic performance and event-related potentials in dyslexic children. PhD thesis, University of Victoria, British Columbia.

Grace GM, Spreen O (1994) Hemisphere-specific stimulation of L and P types: a replication study and a critical appraisal. In Bakker's Balance Model of Dyslexia (eds R Licht, G Spyer), pp 133-81) Assen, The Netherlands: Van Gorcum.

Greatrex JC, Drasdo N (1998) Methods of investigating a visual deficit in dyslexia. Opthalmic Physiological Optics 18, 160-6.

Greenough WT, Juraska JM (1979) Experience-induced changes in brain fine structure: their behavioural implications. In Development and evolution of brain size. Behavioural implications (ed ME Hahn, C Jensen, BC Dudek), (pp 295-320). New York: Academic Press.

Gross-Glenn K, Duari R, Roshii F, Barker WW. Chang JY, Apicella A, Boothe T, Lubs HA (1986) PET scan studies during reading in dyslexic and non-dyslexic adults. Neuroscience Abstracts.

Gross-Glenn K (and 11 others) (1995) Contrast sensitivity in dyslexia. Visual Neuroscience 12, 153-63.

Hogben J (1997) How does a visual transient deficit affect reading? In Dyslexia: biology, cognition and intervention (eds C Hulme, MJ Snowling). London: Whurr.

Holmes B (1994) Fast words speed past dyslexia. New Scientist 27th August, 10.

Hooper SR (1996) Sub-typing specific reading disabilities: classification approaches, recent advances and current status. Mental Retardation and Developmental Disabilities Research Reviews 2, 14-20.

Horwitz B, Rumsey JM, Donohue BC (1998) Functional connectivity of the angular gyrus in normal reading and dyslexia. Proceedings of the National Academy for Science USA 95, 8939-44.

Huettner MIS, Rosenthal BL, Hynd GW (1989) Regional cerebral blood flow (RCBF) in normal readers: bilateral activation with narrative text. Archives of Clinical Neurology 4, 71-8.

Hynd GW (and 9 others) (1995). Dyslexia and corpus callosum morphology. Archives of Neurology 52, 32-8.

Hynd GW, Hynd CR. Sullivan HG, Kingsbury T Jr (1987) Regional cerebral blood flow (RCBF) in developmental dyslexia. Activation during reading in a surface and deep dyslexic. Journal of Learning Disabilities 20, 294-300.

Hynd GW, Marshall RM, Semrud-Clikeman M (1991) Developmental dyslexia, neurolinguistic theory and deviations in brain morphology. Reading and Writing: an Interdisciplinary Journal 3, 345-62.

Hynd GW, Semrud-Clikeman M, Lorys AR, Novey ES, Eliopulos D (1990) Brain morphology in developmental dyslexia and Add/H. Archives of Neurology 47, 919-26.

Johnson OJ, Myklebust HR (1967) Learning disabilities, educational principles and practice. New York: Grune and Stratton.

Johnson MJ, Robertson J (1999) Hemisphere stimulation by computer for pupils with dyslexia. Journal of Learning Disabilities (submitted).

Kappers EJ (1997) Outpatient treatment of dyslexia through stimulation of the cerebral hemispheres. Journal of Learning Disabilities 30 100-25.

Kappers EJ, Bos W (1990) Hemisphere alluding stimulation in two children with dyslexia. Paper presented at the 13th World Congress on Reading, Stockholm, Sweden.

Kappers EJ, Dekker M (1995) Bilingual effects of unilingual neuropsychological treatment of dyslexic adults: a pilot study. Journal of the International Neuropsychological Society 1, 494-500.

Kappers EJ, Hamburger HL (1994) Neuropsychological treatment of dyslexia in out-patients. In The Balance Model of Dyslexia: theoretical and clinical progress (eds R Licht, G Spyer). Assen, The Netherlands: Van Gorcum.

Kinsbourne M (1989) Neuroanatomy of dyslexia. In Neuropsychological correlates and treatment. (eds DJ Bakker and H van der Vlugt). Amsterdam: Swets and Zeitlinger.

Kolb B, Whishaw IQ (1996) Fundamentals of human neuropsychology. New York: Freeman.

Kubova Z, Kuba M, Peregrin J, Navoka V (1996) Visual evoked potential evidence for magnocellular system deficit in dyslexia. Physiological Research 14, 87-9.

Kussmaul A (1877) Disturbances of speech. Cyclopaedia of the Practice of Medicine 14, 581-875.

Lehmkuhle S, Garzia RP, Turner L, Hash T, Baro JA (1993) A defective visual pathway in children with reading disability. New England Journal of Medicine 328, 989-96.

Leonard CM, Voeller KKS, Lombardini LJ (1993) Anomalous cerebral structure in dyslexia revealed with magnetic resonance imaging. Archives of Neurology 50, 461-9.

Licht R (1994) Differences in word recognition between P-and L-type reading disability. In The Balance Model Of Dyslexia: theoretical and clinical progress (eds R Licht, G Spyer). Assen, The Netherlands: Van Gorcum.

Licht R, Kok A, Bakker DJ, Bouma A (1986) Hemispheric distribution of ERP components and word naming in preschool children. Brain and Language 27, 101-16.

Livingstone MS, Rosen GD, Drislane FW, Galaburda AM (1991) Physiological and anatomical evidence for a magnocellular defect in developmental dyslexia. Proceedings of the National Academy for Science USA 28, 7943-7.

Lovegrove W (1996) Dyslexia and a transient/magnocellular pathway deficit: the current situation and future directions. Australian Journal of Psychology 48.

Lovegrove W, Martin F, Slaghuis WI (1986) A theoretical and experimental case for a visual deficit in specific reading disability. Cognitive Neuropsychology 3, 225-67.

Macmillan (1989) The Macmillan Reading Analysis, 2nd edn. Windsor: NFER-Nelson.

McNally KI, Stein JF (1996) Auditory temporal coding in dyslexia. Biological Science 263, 961-5.

Manis FR, Seidenberg MS, Doi LM, McBride-Chang C, Petersen A (1996) On the bases of two sub-types of developmental dyslexia. Cognition 58, 157-95.

Masutto C, Bravar L, Fabbro F (1993) Diagnosis and rehabilitation in childhood dyslexia. A neuropsychological approach. Archivio di Psicologia, Neurologia e Psychiatrie 54, 249-62.

Masutto C, Bravar L, Fabbro F (1994) Neurolonguistic differentiation of children with sub-types of Dyslexia. Journal of Learning Disabilities 27, 520-6.

Mattis S, French JH, Rapin I (1975) Dyslexia in children and young adults: three independent neuro-psychological syndromes. Developmental Medicine and Child Neurology 17, 150-63.

Mesulam MM, Mufson EJ (1985) The insula of Reil in man and monkey: architectonics, connectivity and function. In Cerebral cortex, vol. 4. Association and auditory cortices (eds A Peters, EG Jones), pp 179-226. New York: Plenum Press.

Metsala JL, Stanovich KE, Brown GDA (1998) Regularity effects and the phonological deficit model of reading disabilities: a meta-analytic review. Journal of Educational Psychology 90, 279-93.

Miller SL, Tallal P (1995) A behavioral neuroscience approach to developmental language disorders: evidence for a rapid temporal processing deficit. In Manual of developmental psychology (eds D Cicchetti, DJ Cohen), pp 357-90. New York: Wiley.

Mohr B, Pulvermuller F, Zaidel E (1994) Lexical decision after left, right, bilateral presentation of function words, content words and non-words. Evidence for interhemispheric interaction. Neuropsychologia 32, 105-24.

Morgan AE, Hynd GW (1998) Dyslexia, neurolinguistic activity and anatomical variation in the planum temporale. Neuropsychology Review 8, 79-93.

Morgan WP (1896) A case of congenital word blindness. British Medical Journal 2, 1378.

Morton J (1968) Grammar and computation in language behaviour. CR1113 Progress Report No. VI. University of Michigan.

Neale MD (1989) The Neale Analysis of Reading Ability, 2nd edn. Windsor: NFER-Nelson.

Nicholson RI, Fawcett AJ (1994) Reaction times and dyslexia. Quarterly Journal of Experimental Psychology 47A, 29-48.

Nicholson RI, Fawcett AJ (1996) (see page 27).

Nicholson RI, Fawcett AJ, Moss H, Nicolson MK, Reason R (1998) An early reading intervention study: evaluation and implications. British Journal of Educational Psychology, in press.

Neuvonen M, Rekio-Viinikainen N, Ahonen T, Lyytinen H (1992) Tietokoneele sovelluttu Bakkerin tasapainimalliin perustuva lukemisen kuntoutus. Kielikukko 4, 26-9.

Ojemann GA, Mateer C (1979) Cortical and subcortical organisation of human communication: evidence from stimulation studies. In Neurobiology of social communication in primates: an evolutionary perspective (eds HD Stecklis, MJ Raleigh). New York: Academic Press.

Orton S (1925) Wordblindness in school children. Archives of Neurology and Psychiatry 14, 581-615.

Paulesu E, Frith U, Snowling MJ, Gallagher A, Morton J, Frackoviak RSJ, Frith CD (1996) Is developmental dyslexia a disconnection syndrome? Evidence from PET scanning. Brain 119, 143-57.

Penfield W, Roberts L (1959) Speech and brain mechanisms. Princeton NJ: Princeton University Press.

Petersen SE, Fox MI, Posner I, Mintun M, Raichle ME (1988) Positron emission tomographic studies of single word processing. Nature 331, 585-9.

Posner I, Raichle ME (1994) Images of mind. Scientific American Library Series.

Posner MI (1993) Seeing the mind. Science 262, 673-4.

Pumfrey PD, Reason R (1991) Specific learning difficulties (dyslexia): challenges and responses. Windsor: NFER Nelson.

Rae C, Lee MA, Dixon RM, Blamire AM, Thompson CH, Talcott J, Richardson AJ, Stein JF (1998) Metabolic abnormalities in developmental dyslexia detected by 1H magnetic resonance spectroscopy. Lancet 351, 1849-52.

Renner MJ, Rosenzweig MR (1987) Enriched and impoverished environments. New York: Springer.

Rennie J (1991) Dyslexia: a problem of timing. Scientific American 11, 14.

Richards L, Chiarello C (1995) Depth of associated activation in the cerebral hemispheres: mediated versus direct priming Neuropsychologia 33, 171-9.

Ridder WH 3rd, Borsting E, Cooper M, McNeel B, Huang E (1997) Not all dyslexics are created equal. Optometry, Vision and Science 74, 99-104.

Robertson J (1996) Specific learning difficulties for example dyslexia: differential diagnosis and intervention. PhD thesis, Victoria University of Manchester.

Robertson J (1997) Neuropsychological studies in intervention in dyslexia. A report of recent British studies into differential treatment. Poster presented at the 4th World Congress on Dyslexia, Halkidiki, Greece.

Robertson J (1999) Neuropsychological intervention in dyslexia: two studies on British pupils. Journal of Learning Disabilities, in press.

Rourke BP (1982) Central processing difficulties in children. Towards a developmental neuropsychological model. Journal of Child Neuropsychology 4, 1-8.

Rugg MD, Cox CJ, Doyle MC, Wells T (1995) Event-related potentials and the recollection of low and high frequency words. Neuropsychologia 33, 471-84.

Rumsey JM, Andreason P, Zametkin AJ, Aquino T, King AC, Hamburger SD (1992) Failure to activate the left temperoparietal cortex in dyslexia. An oxygen 15 positron emission tomographic study. Archives of Neurology 49, 527-34.

Russo AE. (1993) Effects of the presence of pathological left handedness indicators on the efficiency of a neuropsychological intervention with low achieving readers. Dissertation, Indiana University of Pennsylvania, Harrisburg, USA.

Schatz J, Hale S, Myerson J (1998) Cerebellar contribution to linguistic processing efficiency revealed by focal damage. Journal of the International Neuropsychological Society 4, 491-501.

Schultz RT (and 10 others) (1994). Brain morphology in normal and dyslexic children: the influence of sex and age. Annals of Neurology 35, 732-42.

Shaywitz BA (and 11 others) (1995) Sex differences in the functional organisation of the brain for language. Nature 373, 607-9.

Shaywitz BA (and 13 others) (1998) Functional disruption in the organisation of the brain for reading in dyslexia. Proceedings of the National Academy for Science USA 95, 2636-41.

Silverberg R, Bentin S, Gaziel T, Obler LK, Albert ML (1979) Shift of visual field preference for English words in native Hebrew speakers. Brain and Language 8, 184-90.

Silverberg,R, Gordon HW, Pollack S, Bentin S (1980) Shift of visual field preference for Hebrew words in native speakers learning to read. Brain and Language 11, 99-105.

Skottun BC, Parke LA (1999) The possible relationship between visual deficits and dyslexia: Examination of a critical assumption. Journal of Learning Disabilities 32, 2-5.

Slaghuis WL, Lovegrove WJ, Davidson JA (1993) Vision and language processing deficits are concurrent in dyslexia. Cortex 29, 601-15.

Slaghuis WL, Pinkus SZ (1993) Visual backward masking in central and peripheral vision in late-adolescent dyslexics. Clinical Vision Sciences 8, 187-99.

Small SL, Kendall Flores D, Noll DC (1998) Different neural circuits subserve reading before and after therapy for acquired dyslexia. Brain and Language 62, 298-308.

Snowling MJ (1995) Phonological processing and developmental dyslexia. Journal of Research in Reading 18, 132-8.

Snowling MJ (1997) Language, phonology and learning to read. Chairman's lecture. 25th anniversary of the British Dyslexia Association, York.

Stanovich KE (1991) Discrepancy definitions of reading disability: has intelligence led us astray? Reading Research Quarterly 26, 7-29.

Stanovich KE, Siegel LS, Gottardo A (1997) Progress in the search for dyslexic sub-types. In Dyslexia: biology, cognition and intervention (eds C Hulme, MJ Snowling). London: Whurr.

Stein JF (1997) How impaired magnocellular processing can cause visual reading errors. 4th World Congress on Dyslexia, Halkidiki, Greece.

Stein JF, Walsh V (1997) To see but not to read; the magnocellular theory of dyslexia. Trends in Neuroscience 20, 147-52.

Talcott JB, Hansen P, Willis OC, Richardson AJ, Stein JF (1997) Specific visual deficits in Dyslexia revealed by temporal processing tasks. 4th World Congress of Dyslexia, Halkidiki, Greece.

Tallal P (1980) Auditory temporal perception, phonics and reading disabilities in children. Brain and Language 9, 182-98.

Tallal P (1997) Language learning impairments: integrating basic science, technology and remediation. Keynote lecture, 4th International Conference of the British Dyslexia Association, York.

Tallal P, Miller SL, Bedi G, Byma G, Wang X, Nagarajan SS, Schreiner C, Jenkins WM, Merzenich MM (1996) Science 271, 81-4.

Travis J (1998) Let the games begin; brain-training video games and stretched speech may help language impaired kids and dyslexics. Science News 149, 104-11.

Van Patten C, Rheinfelder H (1995) Conceptual relationships between spoken words and environmental sounds: event-related brain potential measures. Neuropsychologia 33, 485-508.

Walker C (1974) Reading development and extension. London: Ward Lock Educational.

Watson C, Willows DM (1993) Evidence for a visual-processing deficit subtype among disabled readers. In Visual processes in reading and reading disabilities (eds DM Willows, RS Kruk, E Marcos). Hillsdale, NJ: Lawrence Erlbaum.

Wechsler D (1976) Wechsler Intelligence Scale for Children-Revised. Windsor: NFER.

Willerman L (1991) Brains: is bigger better? Science 254, 1584.

Index